CW00751286

FORD MODEL T
AN ENTHUSIAST'S GUIDE

Porter Press International

COVER IMAGE: **Ford Model T.** *(Getty Images)*

Dedication
To Di, the JPs and Will

First published February 2021

ISBN 978 1 913089 22 1

Published by Porter Press International Ltd

Hilltop Farm, Knighton-on-Teme,
Tenbury Wells, WR15 8LY, UK
Tel: +44 (0)1584 781588
sales@porterpress.co.uk
www.porterpress.co.uk

Project manager: Steve Rendle
Copy editor: Beth Dymond
Proof reader: Dean Rockett
Indexer: Peter Nicholson
Page design: James Robertson/Martin Port
Printed by Gomer Press Ltd

COPYRIGHT

Bibliography

Publications
The Story of the Race: How the Ford Car won the Transcontinental Contest for the Guggenheim Trophy, told by one of the crew on Ford Car No.1, 1959 reprint of 1909 original, published by the Ford Motor Company

The Ford Model T Car, by Victor W Pagé, published by the Norman W Henley Publishing Company, 1917

Farewell to Model T, by Richard Lee Strout and E B White, published by G P Putnams Sons, 1936

Henry Ford, a biography, by William Adams Simonds, published by Michael Joseph Ltd, 1946

History of the Motor Car, by Marco Matteucci, published by New English Library, 1970

On Four Wheels, Volume Three, Graham Gauld and others, Published by Orbis Publishing, 1976-1977

The Ford in Britain File – Model by Model, by Eric Dymock, published by Dove Publishing, 2002

The Model T – A Centennial History, by Robert Casey, published by John Hopkins University Press, 2008

Model T Ford Factory Service Manual (reprint), by Ford Motor Company and David Grant Stewart Sr (Editor), 2012

Le Mans – The official history of the world's greatest motor race, 1923-29, by Quentin Spurring, published by Evro, 2015.

Model T Ford Questions and Answers (reprint), by Ford Motor Company and David Grant Stewart Sr (Editor), 2016

Henry Ford, A Life from Beginning to End, Hourly History, 2017

The Bronze Ford, compiled by Neil Tuckett and Flora Seddon, 2018

A Brief History of the Model T Ford, by Jon Branch, published on silodrome.com, 2018

Colonel Stephens and his Railmotors, by Brian Janes and Ross Shimmon, published by Lightmoor Press, 2018

The Entire Life Story of Henry Ford, The History Hour, 2019

Websites
Wikipedia
racingsportscars.com
thehenryford.com
Michigan Motor Sports Hall of Fame (mmshof.org)
modeltfordfix.com
digitaslcollections.lib.washington.edu
hemmings.com
museumofamericanspeed.com
modelt.ca
speedsters.com
colonelstephenssociety.co.uk
voxy.co.nz
modeltford.co.nz
landships.info
National Library of Medicine (pubmed.ncbi.nlm.nih.gov)
Autoweek.com
History.com

FORD MODEL T
AN ENTHUSIAST'S GUIDE
1908 TO 1927 (ALL MODELS AND VARIANTS)

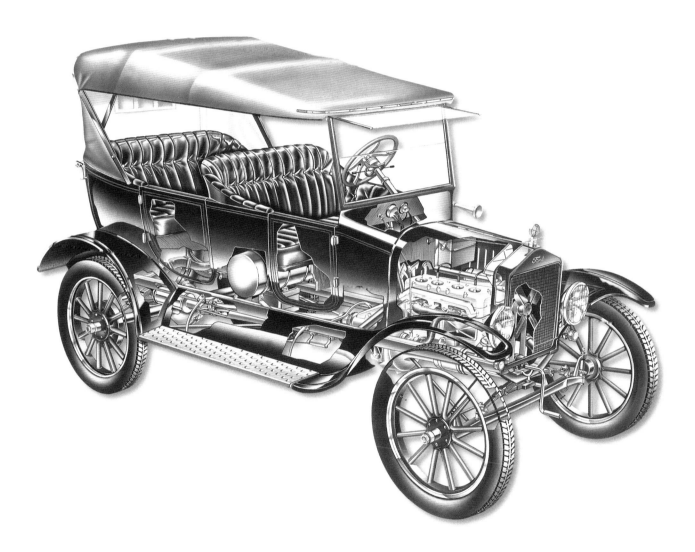

An insight into the design, production and ownership of the car that introduced motoring to the masses

Chas Parker

With contributions from Chris Barker and Neil Tuckett

Contents

OPPOSITE **A Model T Ford leaves the London showrooms of Ford UK at 55–59 Shaftesbury Avenue, circa 1914.** *(Getty Images)*

Introduction

In his 1945 novel, *Cannery Row*, the Nobel Prize-winning author John Steinbeck wrote: 'Someone should write an erudite essay on the moral, physical, and aesthetic effect of the Model T Ford on the American nation.' This book is not that essay.

Steinbeck continued:

Two generations of Americans knew more about the Ford coil than the clitoris, about the planetary system of gears than the solar system of stars. With the Model T, part of the concept of private property disappeared. Pliers ceased to be privately owned and a tire pump belonged to the last man who had picked it up. Most of the babies of the period were conceived in Model T Fords and not a few were born in them...

I'm not sure that records exist that would prove or disprove the validity of that last statement, but it is true to say that the Model T Ford transformed American society and then proceeded to spread its influence across the globe. The very fact that Steinbeck singled it out is testament to that.

Consider the following: in 1914, Ford made more cars than all the other manufacturers combined.

By 1918 half of all the cars in the US were Model Ts, and by the time the ten millionth car rolled off the production line, half of all the cars in the world were Fords. In 1925, production was at a rate of about 8,000 cars per day – that's two million a year. In total, over 15 million Model Ts were made, a figure only surpassed in 1972 by the VW Beetle.

So what was it about this instantly recognisable design that gave it such mass appeal? I suppose you have to say that Henry Ford got it right first time. He produced a vehicle that fitted all the requirements of the day. It was simple, affordable, reliable and designed to deal with the appalling road conditions prevalent in America at that time; and having got it right, he didn't bother to change it.

Having said that, start looking at photos of Model T Fords and you'll soon realise that there is no such thing as a definitive model. The chassis and running gear remain the same but the bodies are all different. There's the Touring, the Roadster, the Torpedo Runabout, the Centredoor, the Flatbed Truck – the list goes on and on. Yet each one is unmistakably a Model T Ford. And that's the other thing that helps explain its popularity and longevity – it was flexible. The Model T could be used as a basis for all sorts of uses, both private and commercial. Ford, seeing this, introduced the Ton Truck and expanded his market even further.

The car became famous in popular culture as well, becoming synonymous with the likes of Laurel and Hardy and the Keystone Cops. Everywhere you looked in the 1920s, there was a Model T Ford of one sort or another.

BELOW Norman Rockwell's painting of a Model T Ford – *A Sunday Afternoon Farm Scene*, 1910. *(Ford Images)*

It didn't last, of course. Nothing does. Ford's approach to the Model T had been to get it right and then not alter it significantly. He believed it was the only car people would ever need. But as other manufacturers offered more enhancements and comforts, the appeal of the Model T gradually fell. Even so, today there are thought to be around 50,000 or more examples still running, lovingly tended to by their owners and kept running through specialist suppliers. There's no shortage of spare parts.

As always, this book could not have been written without the help of others, all of whom are far more knowledgeable about the subject than I am, and, despite the difficulties presented by the COVID-19 situation, were all willing to share their enthusiasm and expertise with me.

Special mention must be made of Neil Tuckett and Chris Barker, who willingly gave their time and showed great patience in fact-checking and correcting my text for me.

Finally, thanks must go to my partner, Diane Murphy, for writing the Henry Ford biography and for continuing love, support, encouragement and wine.

Chas Parker
October 2020

Acknowledgements

Chris Barker, archivist, Model T Register of
   Great Britain
Warren Crone, Ford Images
Jon Day, National Motor Museum
Linda Freedman, Thumbs Up Video
   Productions LLC
Mike Hallowes, Ten Tenths
Brian Janes, Kent & East Sussex Railway
Ian Morgan
Rob McKenzie, Model T Ford Club of New
   Zealand
Carla Reczek, Detroit Public Library
Steve Rendle
Richard Rimmer, The T Service
Richard Skinner, Tudor Wheels
John Stokes
Neil Tuckett, Tuckett Brothers

ABOVE **Stan Laurel (left) and Oliver Hardy in the 1928 James Parrott/MGM film,** *Two Tars*. *(Getty Images)*

BELOW **The Model T Ford had mass appeal and was put to all number of different uses, but quite what this represents is difficult to imagine.** *(NMM)*

Chapter One

The Model T story

'I will build a vehicle for the great multitude. It will be large enough for the family, but small enough for the individual to run and care for. It will be constructed of the best materials, by the best men to be hired, after the simplest designs that modern engineering can devise. But it will be so low in price that no man making a good salary will be unable to own one – and enjoy with his family the blessing of hours of pleasure in God's great open spaces.'

Henry Ford

PREVIOUS SPREAD **One thousand Model T chassis, the result of just one nine-hour shift in August 1913, sit outside the Ford factory in Highland Park, Michigan.** *(Ford Images)*

BELOW Henry Ford's first car, a Quadricycle, built in 1896. *(Ford Images)*

L et's start with a few figures to put things into context. The Model T Ford was produced between 1 October 1908 and 26 May 1927, with around 15.9 million examples being sold. It was the first mass-produced car using moving assembly lines and interchangeable components. At a time when the horse and the railroad were the only really viable means of land travel, Henry Ford brought mobility through car ownership to millions of middle-class people. He also decided to market his product at a time when supplies of fuel and oil were not widespread and few roads were graded or surfaced.

Ford was working as the chief engineer at the Detroit Edison Electric Illuminating Company when he built his first automobile, a Quadricycle, in 1896, in a brick shed behind his house. He had already spent many hours trying to perfect an engine that would run on petrol and now he wanted to see if he could use it to power a four-wheeled carriage.

In his biography of Henry Ford, published in 1946, William Adams Simonds describes that first Ford car:

When possible, parts were made from scrap-metal, machined on the lathe and worked with the tools. The two-cylinders were bored and fitted in sections of the exhaust pipe of a steam engine. The crankshaft was forged at the Detroit Dry Docks works, where Mr Ford had learned his apprenticeship under [Frank E] Kirby. Charles B King, who had built a horseless carriage of his own, back in 1894, contributed two intake valves.

Four bicycle wheels about 28 inches in diameter comprised the car's running gear. The steering device was a tiller attached to the front wheels; the driver warned traffic by means of an alarm gong. A simple bicycle saddle, mounted on the three-gallon fuel tank, provided a seat. A buggy seat wide enough for two came later.

To transmit the engine's power to the countershaft he arranged two belts which

gave the driver a choice of speeds – ten or twenty miles an hour. One belt ran off the periphery of the flywheel; the other came from a much smaller wheel on the right face of the flywheel. When a driver pushed a lever forward it put the belt on high speed; when back, it was low; when upright, in neutral. A chain connected the countershaft to the rear wheels. There was no reverse – and there were no brakes.

Ford sold that first car to Charles Ainsley of Detroit for $200, and thereby set in motion the concept of a light and economical automobile that would eventually culminate in the Model T.

That same year, Charles and Frank Duryea, the first Americans to design and build a series of cars for sale, made and sold 13 cars through their Duryea Motor Wagon Company, but it closed its doors two years later. Other companies followed, such as the Winton Motor Carriage Company and the Haynes-Apperson Company, and by 1908 there were 166 manufacturers of cars in the US – 151 of which made vehicles powered by the internal combustion engine burning petrol – while there were just 11 electric car manufacturers and four making steam-powered cars.

The types of cars could be divided roughly into three groups: the first being what was known as the 'Mercedes' type, with the engine mounted behind the front axle, allowing the chassis to be low, and capable of cruising at 50mph (80kph) over good roads, such as those found in Europe.

American roads, on the other hand, were mainly dirt, which became dusty in hot weather and mud baths when it rained. This had led to the development of what was known as 'high-wheelers' – cars with a high chassis mounted onto wide, wooden wheels with solid rubber tyres, and the engine mounted at the rear. Truly 'horseless carriages'.

The third type were known as 'runabouts', which were essentially a smaller version of the 'Mercedes' type, with small front-mounted engines.

Ford built a second car two years after his first and then, in 1899, he left his job with the Detroit Edison Electric Illuminating Company and, together with a group of investors, formed

the Detroit Automobile Company, whose first and only product was a petrol-powered delivery truck, completed in January 1900. Ford, however, was not happy with the design of the 'mixer', or carburettor, and refused to allow the vehicle to be put into production until he was satisfied that he had perfected it. This frustrated his investors and Ford parted company with them after just a year.

As Simonds wrote in his 1946 biography:

The termination of his connection with that first company revealed a characteristic of his that continued unchanged throughout his later career. While developing a new model or working on an engineering design he would not be hurried nor persuaded to release it for production until he was entirely satisfied with it. Executives might tear their hair, dealers might plead that competitors were stealing the market, but nothing could budge him. The first stockholders of the first company discovered that fact, and found that rather than yield to them he preferred to break connections.

He then briefly formed the Henry Ford Company in 1901, but disagreements over the time he was spending developing his racing cars (see Chapter Six) meant that he also left that in 1902, albeit retaining the rights to the Ford name. After his departure, the company became the Cadillac Automobile Company.

Undeterred, Ford briefly went into partnership with Tom Cooper, a champion bicycle racer of the time, to build two racing cars. One of them, driven by pioneer automobile racer Barney Oldfield and named '999' after a famous locomotive of the New York Central and Hudson River Railroad, went on to win the Manufacturers' Challenge Cup at Grosse Pointe, Michigan, on 25 October 1902, just days after Ford had sold his share of the partnership to Cooper.

Nevertheless, Oldfield's and Cooper's continuing success with the car helped to establish Ford's reputation as an automobile designer, which led to him attracting the backing of Alexander Y. Malcomson, a wealthy coal dealer. Together they formed Ford and Malcomson, but this was short-lived and new investors joined in, including John and Horace Dodge. The company was reformed as the Ford Motor Company on

16 June 1903, with Ford as vice-president, head of engineering and general manager.

The company's first vehicles were the two-cylinder Models A, C and F, released in 1903, 1904 and 1905, respectively. These were typical of the early 'horseless carriages' in that the engines were mounted underneath the seats with a chain drive to the rear wheels.

Ford and Malcomson, however, disagreed about the direction the company should take; Malcomson favouring the production of large, expensive vehicles, while Ford wanted to produce smaller, inexpensive models that ordinary people could afford. Malcomson, together with four other shareholders, wanted to press ahead with a four-cylinder Model B,

RIGHT **1903 Ford Model A.** *(Ford Images)*

costing $2,000, and a six-cylinder Model K, priced at $2,500. Ford, plus six other shareholders, favoured the four-cylinder Model N, intended to be sold for just $500.

In order to outmanoeuvre his opponents within the company, in November 1905, Ford formed the Ford Manufacturing Company, in which Malcomson and his allies were not involved. The company made parts for the Model N and sold them to the Ford Motor Company at a price that meant profits on the car were very low. Ford and his companions enjoyed the profits from the manufacturing company, but Malcomson had very little income from either the Model N or the slow-selling K. The result of all this was that Malcomson

ABOVE **1906 Ford Model N.** *(Ford Images)*

LEFT **1906 Ford Model K Touring.** *(Ford Images)*

eventually sold out to Ford in July 1906, followed by his supporters, and in the following year the now-redundant Ford Manufacturing Company ceased trading.

Ford's Model N became very successful and was described by *Cycle and Automobile Trade Journal* as 'distinctly the most important mechanical traction event of 1906'. The 'runabout'-style Model N featured a four-cylinder, 15hp engine, giving the two-seater vehicle a top speed of around 45mph (72kph), and it was priced at $500, far lower than its competitors. Built in parallel to the 'N', and using the same chassis, were the Models 'R' and 'S', but these were still of the 'runabout' style and could accommodate at most three passengers. Ford wanted something aimed at the middle classes, which would provide

reliable and comfortable transport for a family of four at an affordable price and could cope with the challenging conditions of many of the American roads of the time.

The first design requirement was for the car to be light. Ford had been intrigued by the advantages of using vanadium alloy steel, which was stronger than standard carbon steel. In 1907 he had adopted the alloy for the

Sectioned view of 1920 Ford Model T engine. Simple, durable, easy to maintain and cheap, the Model T engine remained essentially unchanged from its introduction until the car was replaced by the Model A in 1927. It was a four-cylinder, 2.9-litre (177-cu in), 20hp, side valve engine, which gave the car a maximum speed of 40mph (64kph). It was also used as a power plant for specialist vehicles and other applications. Such was its usefulness that it continued in production for marine and industrial purposes until 1931, and thence in batch production until 1941. *(SSPL/Getty Images)*

production of axles and gears in the Model N and Model K. When the new car, designated the Model T, appeared in 1908, it weighed just 1,200lb (544kg) – far lighter than any other four-seater car available at the time.

By this time, Ford had built a team of automotive engineers around him, including Childe Harold Wills, Joseph A Galamb, Eugene Farkas, Henry Love, CJ Smith, Gus Degner, Peter E Martin, Charles E. Sorensen and William K Knudsen, and it was their combined expertise and vision that resulted in the Model T Ford.

The four-cylinder, 2.9-litre (177-cu in) engine featured a one-piece cylinder block with detachable cylinder head. This contrasted with other car engines of the time that comprised cylinders either cast singly or in pairs, often with fixed cylinder heads, which were then bolted to a separate crankcase – a process that made them large and expensive to produce. Ford's engine produced 20hp, which, given the light weight of the car, produced more than adequate performance.

Another innovation was in the front suspension. Most cars utilised a pair of leaf springs mounted longitudinally, whereas the Model T featured a single spring, mounted transversely above the front axle. This, combined with the light, flexible chassis and high ground clearance of 10in (25cm), meant that the car could cope with the poor road conditions and deep ruts, the axle and wheels moving with the contours of the road. The rear axle employed a similar arrangement.

Instead of opting for a sliding gear change, Ford decided that, from the driver's point of view, an easy-to-shift, planetary transmission system would be far simpler, even though it restricted the Model T to just two forward speeds.

There was more pioneering engineering in the form of the flywheel magneto, which provided the electricity to ignite the fuel-air mixture. The magneto was built into the flywheel, which carried 16 vee-shaped permanent magnets. Mounted at the rear of the engine were a corresponding 16 wire coils arranged in a circle. As the flywheel revolved, the magnetic field of the magnets passed through the stationary coils, generating the electric current that powered 'trembler coils', the devices that produced the high voltage needed by the spark plugs.

By October 1907, two prototype Model Ts had been built at the Piquette Avenue production plant and development on the car continued for another year. In late September 1908, Ford drove one of the prototype Model Ts from Detroit to Iron Mountain in Michigan, via Chicago and Milwaukee, a round trip of 1,357 miles (2,184km). The company's own publication, *Ford Times*, reported: 'The roads going were six inches deep in dust – returning after the rains the roads were wet and muddy, and the car when it arrived in Detroit looked as if it had been taking a mud bath.'

The first production Model T, which Ford kept for himself, was built on 12 August 1908 and left the factory on 27 September. Numbers two to nine were immediately shipped to London for the Motor Show at Olympia on 13 November, where the car made its public debut, and then on to the Paris Motor Show. Within days of its announcement, 15,000 orders were placed.

The first 2,500 production cars used a gear-driven pump to circulate the water but after this a thermosyphon system was employed in which the water circulated naturally, due to it being hotter in the engine than in the radiator. It was another example of Ford's desire to keep things as simple as possible. He once said: 'The less

complex an article, the easier it is to make, the cheaper it may be sold, and therefore the greater number may be sold.'

Another change after the first 2,500 models had been built was the use of thicker steel for the chassis frames. The original thickness of steel had proved to be too light, and reinforcing plates had to be riveted inside the rails of the frame of the first 2,500 models. Early Model Ts also had 'two-lever' controls, a significant difference from later cars (see Chapter Two).

By 1910, 12,000 Model Ts had been produced and Ford was struggling to keep up with demand.

Assembly process

Ford's key to rapid production and cost control was the efficient handling of materials, the sequential arrangement of machine tools and single-purpose machines, the use of fully interchangeable parts and the efficient use of the station assembly process.

The various sub-assemblies, such as dashboards, engines, transmissions and axles, were brought together at specially designed benches or assembly stations, which included storage for all the necessary individual parts. A team of workers assembled one section before moving on to the next chassis, leaving another team to carry out the next stage.

In 1913 Ford radically streamlined the assembly process to increase output with the introduction of 'moving line assembly'. He apparently got the idea from the slaughterhouses of Chicago, where workers specialised in a single task, repeating it over and over as a conveyor belt of carcasses moved slowly past them. These were known as 'dis-assembly lines'. At the new Highland Park factory, a production team comprising Childe Harold Wills, Clarence Avery, Peter F. Martin and Charles E. Sorensen devised a moving assembly production line process, one of the first of which was for the flywheels, where workers attached the V-shaped magnets to form one half of the flywheel magneto.

Productivity immediately increased and, according to *The Model T: A Centennial History* by Robert Casey, 'Twenty-nine workers produced flywheels at a rate of one every thirteen minutes and ten seconds per person, compared to twenty minutes per person under the station assembly system.'

The assembly line process was quickly adopted throughout the Highland Park plant, replacing all the station assembly stands. It meant that the build time for a Model T dropped from 12½ hours to 93 minutes by 1914. The moving assembly line also meant the cost of a Model T was kept low. Ford decreased the price of the car over the years, dropping from $825 in 1908 to $360 by 1916, in the belief that increased demand would result in lower unit cost, which it did.

In 1909, Ford built 13,842 cars. In 1910, the first year of the Highland Park plant, this had risen to 20,748 for the year. In 1911 it was 54,001; in 1912, 94,663; in 1913, 224,784; and in 1914, 248,916.

BELOW **Exterior of the Highland Park factory.** *(Alamy)*

FACTORIES

The first Ford Motor Company plant was a rented building on Mack Avenue, Detroit and was in operation from 1903–04. Originally a single-storey building, it was expanded with a second floor at the end of 1903. It was used to assemble the Models A and C. Components were bought in and production was by the process of 'station assembly', with each car put together in one place by a single team. This system of hand-building a car piece by piece meant that in the first month just 11 cars were constructed.

The second factory was located on the corner of Piquette and Beaubien Avenues in Detroit. This was the first to be built and owned by the company. It was three stories tall and 63,000ft^2 (5,850m^2)in area. The building was used from 1904 to 1910. The building now houses a Ford museum, run by volunteers.

The Ford Manufacturing Company, which manufactured the parts for the Model N, was housed at 773–775 Bellevue Avenue. In 1907 the Ford Manufacturing Company was absorbed by the Ford Motor Company and all production was centralised at the Piquette Avenue site.

In summer 1906, the company bought land in Highland Park, north of Detroit, and construction of a new factory began in 1908. A feature of this new facility was a monorail

BELOW Drawing of Ford Piquette plant.
(Ford Images)

system for moving material through the plant, which opened in 1910. The monorail track ran for over a mile-and-a-half through the factory, connecting the foundry, heat-treatment buildings and machine shops, allowing sequential operations at each stage of manufacture.

With sales in the United Kingdom flourishing, in October 1911, Ford opened an assembly plant at Trafford Park, Manchester. The first British Model T assembled from parts shipped from the US was produced on 23 October 1911, but by the 1920s components were produced in-house. The new assembly line process developed in the US was introduced to the new plant and between 1912 and 1913 output doubled from 3,000 to 6,000 cars. In total, 300,000 Model Ts were built at the Trafford Park facility. It was the largest car factory in Europe at the time and also supplied components to the other European Ford assembly plants.

In 1917 Ford began construction of an even larger facility in Detroit, on marshland, close to where the Rouge and Detroit rivers merged. The new facility included blast furnaces, coal ovens, steel furnaces, rolling mills, stamping plants – everything required to manufacture complete cars from scratch. A dedicated engine manufacturing and assembly building was built,

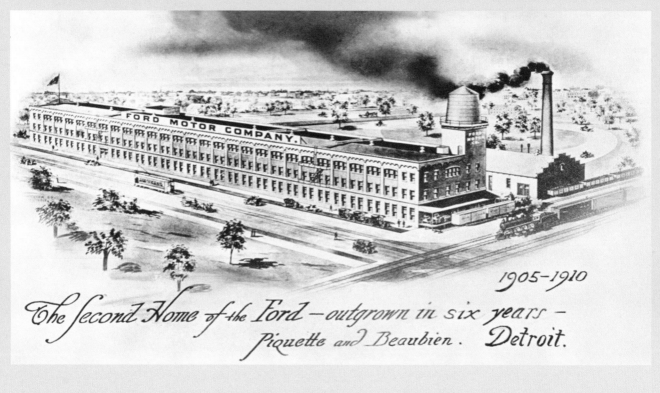

The Second Home of the Ford – outgrown in six years –
Piquette and Beaubien. Detroit. 1905–1910

and castings were made in the world's largest foundry. The whole facility was connected by a network of monorails, tramways, conveyor belts and 93 miles of railways.

Although many parts for the Model T were manufactured at the new Rouge facility up until 1927, final assembly still took place at Highland Park and branches. Sales and production had peaked in 1923 as tastes had changed and the car-buying public demanded more comfort and style, and Ford was facing stiff competition from companies such as General Motors and Chrysler.

ABOVE The Highland Park facility, 1920. *(Ford Images)*

BELOW The 250,000th Model T Ford produced at Manchester, 1925. Management and workers pose with the car to commemorate this production milestone. The hugely successful Model T was Britain's best-selling car from 1913 to 1923. The factory began assembling cars from imported parts in 1911, but by 1924 the vehicles were being constructed from 94% British parts. In 1931, Ford switched its manufacturing activities to its massive new plant at Dagenham, Essex. *(Photo by National Motor Museum/Heritage Images/Getty Images)*

RIGHT An obviously posed photograph, apparently of the Highland Park assembly line. The worker at the front appears to be using a large wrench on the flimsy, pressed hubcap, which in reality would not tolerate anything beyond being tightened by hand. Notice also the white-painted engine and ancillaries, which possibly indicate that this was a special-edition Model T, such as the 10-millionth or 15-millionth car to come off the production line. *(Alamy)*

ABOVE 1914 Highland Park fuel tank installation. *(Ford Images)*

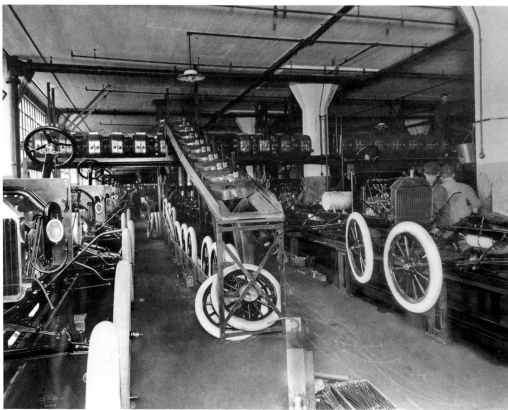

RIGHT 1914 Highland Park radiators on chute. *(Ford Images)*

ABOVE 1917 engine assembly. *(Ford Images)*

LEFT 1913 Highland Park engine installation. A 'push type' assembly line at the Highland Park plant in Michigan. The photograph shows a Model T engine being dropped into place by use of an overhead block and tackle. The picture was taken in early 1913 and it shows how the rear wheels were cradled in a three-wheel dolly which moved along a track on the floor. Cars were pushed from one station to another for assembling. *(Alamy)*

RIGHT 1913 Highland Park magneto installation. This was one of the first processes to utilise the new moving assembly line. *(Ford Images)*

BELOW bodies being delivered to Highland Park in 1915. The bodies were made by Briggs Manufacturing and arrived unpainted and unupholstered. The inclined conveyor belt in the centre of the picture carries the bodies into the factory. *(Ford Images)*

ABOVE **1923 Highland Park assembly line.** *(Ford Images)*

LEFT **1914 Highland Park Model T assembly.** *(Alamy)*

BELOW **1914 Highland Park Model T assembly.** *(Alamy)*

The increased productivity was not popular with the workers though, and turnover of the labour force rose to 380% by late 1913. To combat this, in 1914, Ford took the extraordinary step of raising the pay from $2.34 for a nine-hour day, to $5.00 for an eight-hour day. Workers were subjected to an investigation into their private lives in order to be deemed qualified for the new wage, but the enticement was so great that it outweighed this intrusion and the monotony of the repetitive assembly line work.

To keep up with increasing demand for the Model T, in 1914 the Highland Park facility was expanded with the addition of two new six-storey buildings, 842ft long and 62ft wide (256m x 19m). By 1917 these had been joined by another two similar buildings. Ford's model years usually ran from August of the previous year, so production of 1917 cars began in August 1916.

In 1919 Henry Ford bought out all his minority shareholders and became sole owner of the Ford Motor Company.

Ford gradually took more and more of the production process in-house, manufacturing glass for windscreens, cloth and artificial leather

for the folding tops, a plastic known as Fordite for the steering wheel rims, bearings, wire and batteries.

'It was a huge operation,' explains Neil Tuckett of UK Model T specialists, Tuckett Brothers. 'The whole scale was incredible and they got good at it. The other thing was that, whereas with the normal car manufacturer a man did a job, Ford built a machine to do a job that was operated by a man. And that's really the big difference as I see it.

'A lot of the off-cuts, from wings and whatever, were reused – there was no waste. One of the wing off-cuts was used for clutch plates, and you know how good a clutch plate has got to be, so you know there's quality in it. Half the cars in the world were Model Ts at one point, so half the drivers in the world were Model T drivers.'

Ford began to export cars to Great Britain, Germany, Belgium and Mexico and an assembly plant was opened in Canada in 1904. This was followed by similar plants in Great Britain (1911); France (1913); Argentina (1916); Denmark (1919); Spain and Uruguay (1920); Italy and Belgium (1922); South Africa (1924); Japan, Australia and Mexico (1925); and Germany, Malaya and India (1926). The Canadian plant began manufacture rather than just assembly, and cars were shipped partly assembled from there and Detroit to the plants around the world, where final assembly took place.

BELOW 1914 final assembly. *(Ford Images)*

Marketing

In 1914, Ford offered to provide a rebate to Model T buyers if sales of the car exceeded 300,000 the following year. On 15 August 1915, it was announced that sales had reached 308,213 and that each buyer would receive a cheque for $50. It cost the Ford Motor Company $15,410,650 but Henry Ford regarded it as money well spent. In fact, all the publicity that Ford was receiving meant that it could afford to cease all national advertising for almost six and a half years between 1917 and 1923, relying solely on advertising by Ford dealerships. The car was so famous, it was simply regarded as the norm, and Henry Ford claimed that the savings in advertising were passed on to the car buyer.

Decline of the Model T

Sales of the Model T peaked in 1921 when Ford held a 60% share of the US car market. Absolute sales peaked in 1923, with over 1.8 million cars sold, but sales slowly declined thereafter.

There were a number of contributary reasons to the gradual decline in popularity of the Model T. For a start, Ford did not keep pace with technological advances offered by other manufacturers. Items such as the six-volt dynamo, starter and battery didn't become available on Fords until 1919 and not as standard fittings until 1926.

Cooling systems that used water pumps as opposed to the Model T's thermosyphon system were now just as reliable and less likely to boil over. The sliding gear transmission overtook the Model T's two-speed planetary transmission, the main disadvantage of which was the need to keep the slow pedal pushed firmly down all the time the car was in slow-moving traffic or climbing steep hills.

When Ford introduced a closed body for the Model T, it increased the 1,200lb (544kg)car into a top-heavy 1,950lb (885kg) one, rendering it more sluggish. Improvements in the road system also meant that the T's high ground clearance, short wheelbase and flexible three-point suspension were no longer necessary.

PAINT IT BLACK

Although it is true that, for a while, Model T Fords were only available in black, in fact only about 11.5 million out of 15 million of them were, and many other colours were also available over its lifetime, including grey, red and green, dependent on the body style.

Early 1909 Model Ts were red, grey or dark green. In mid-1909 they were all dark green, followed by all midnight blue with black fenders in 1911, both of which appear black in early monochrome photographs, compounding the idea that all the cars were this colour. Then, in 1912, Henry Ford uttered the phrase which has become synonymous with the Model T: 'Any customer can have a car painted any colour that he wants so long as it is black', which has been abbreviated over the years to 'any colour you like as long as it's black'. The policy was implemented with black as the standard colour until, in August 1925, a choice of colours was reintroduced to try to combat falling sales.

It is still debated as to whether Henry Ford chose black as the single option colour because it dried faster than other colours, or because it was more durable and less expensive than other paints. After the reintroduction of colours, areas of the car subject to high wear, such as the fenders and running boards, were still painted black due to its durability. It must also have helped simplify and streamline the production process to offer a single colour.

Neil Tuckett is convinced he knows why black was chosen, though. 'Black was used predominantly because it was the fastest drying paint, is the main reason as far as I'm concerned,' he said. 'There may have been other reasons, but it worked.'

The emergence of a consumer society, where people had more disposable income, meant that their expectations were higher and items once regarded as luxuries were now deemed commonplace. Car owners not only wanted comfort and convenience, they now wanted style as well as speed. By 1923 this was one of the most important factors. Car manufacturers began to change the style of their models on an annual basis in order to entice car owners to trade in their two- or three-year-old car for the latest version. The Model T began to be less attractive than its rivals.

'The car had changed a lot, but the concept hadn't,' explains Neil Tuckett. 'By the mid-twenties they were dated. They were losing out to competitors who had four-wheel brakes, three-speed gearboxes and were more comfortable. But Ford was very keen to keep his baby going.'

Ford tried cutting prices, which had always worked for him in the past, slashing the cost of a Model T to $290 and bringing profits on car sales down to just $2 per car, but to no avail. Ford hid his head in the sand and resisted replacing the Model T for as long as he could, despite opposition from others within the company, including from his son Edsel. In 1926 he was still saying: 'The Ford car is a tried and proved product that requires no tinkering.'

Even so, in October 1925, he had introduced the 'Improved' Model T for the following year. This offered a complete restyling, with all-steel bodies, lowered chassis, nickel-plated radiator and new colour options on the closed cars. 'The fuel tank was moved from under the seat to under the bulkhead, so you had better gravity feed,' explains Neil Tuckett, 'and they had competition, so they reintroduced colours and put a bit more nickel on things, to spruce them up. Before that, it was just a black car with either a brass or black radiator. The very last of

them had nickel-plated radiators.'

According to *The Essential Buyer's Guide: Ford Model T* by Chris Barker and Neil Tuckett, it is a myth that Henry Ford refused to change the Model T at all over its 19-year production life. He resisted replacing the car but did change many components. The new ones were largely interchangeable with the old, meaning that some Model Ts can have parts of varying age. 'If you take a 1909 and a 1927 car, 20 years apart, you could just swap engines or swap axles, and you could still keep that car on the road,' said Neil Tuckett. 'You would update it, but they were pretty interchangeable. The rolling chassis was basically the same throughout, other than technical improvements.'

Production of the Model T came to a symbolic end on 26 May 1927, when Edsel and Henry Ford drove out of the Highland Park plant in the 15 millionth Model T. Nearly half a million more were assembled around the world, but this was where production of the car finished.

BELOW Henry Ford stands alongside the ten millionth Model T to roll off the production line, together with his first Quadricycle.
(Alamy)

Ford said:

The Model T was a pioneer. There was no conscious public need of motor cars when we first made it. There were few good roads. This car blazed the way for the motor industry and started the movement for good roads everywhere. It is still the pioneer car in many parts of the world which are just beginning to be motorised. But conditions in this country have so greatly changed that further refinement in motor car construction is desirable, and our new model is a recognition of this.

The Model T Ford was succeeded by the Model A. The rest of the history of the Ford Motor Company has already been well documented and is too extensive for inclusion here, but suffice to say it is still one of the world's leading automobile manufacturers.

ABOVE The 15 millionth Model T coming off the assembly line at the Dearborn factory, 26 May 1927. *(Getty Images)*

BELOW Edsel and Henry Ford stand alongside Ford's first Quadricycle and the 15 millionth Model T, 30 June 1927. *(Alamy)*

By Diane Murphy

Passionate innovator, pacifist, idealist, anti-Semitic, dogmatic, controlling, philanthropist, bully, social liberator, inflexible pedant, visionary, welfare capitalist – all of these words and indeed many more can be used to describe the undoubted genius that was Henry Ford. For the purposes of this book, let us just stick with the story of his life.

Born in 1863, Henry Ford was the first child of William Ford and his wife Mary. Over the next ten years there were to be four more children born to this loving and hard-working couple. William's father John had moved his family from Ireland and emigrated to America 16 years earlier, and 12 years after that William met and courted Mary Litogot.

John worked hard and after a decade he turned rented land into a successful farm at Dearborn, just outside Detroit. By 1858,

BELOW **Henry Ford.**
(Alamy)

encouraged by his father's example and his own fierce work ethic, William had saved enough money to buy land from his father in Greenfield Township. Once love had blossomed with Mary he set about building a large and impressive family home for his new wife and her adoptive parents, which was completed in 1861. Often described as a workaholic, William prospered and became respected in their community, but there is little doubt that Mary, with her loving ways, was the fabric that bound this family together.

Devoted wife and loving mother, Mary nurtured and supported her family, but her special and strongest bond was with her first born, Henry. It was an idyllic childhood. From their father they learnt a good work ethic, a love and respect of nature and a deep understanding of how the land worked. From their mother they learnt to read (they could all read before they went to school) but also to be fair, kind, enquiring and diligent. Henry also wanted to know why, how, and what if? Thus, armed with both the mental and physical confidence with which his parents had equipped him, Henry was set for a great childhood. No greater gift.

Henry went to school at the age of seven, where he was taught by rote. No place for either innovation or an enquiring mind. At the age of nine he was sent to the Miller School in Dearborn where he started to experiment and explore. His early fascination was with how steam worked, and not all forays into this science went well. One notable occasion was when he filled a pan with water, tied the lid on and set it on the fire. The resulting explosion and scalding was nowhere near as painful as the scolding he received from his mother. Another time he enlisted the help of classmates at school. This explosion ended in the school fence burning down. Though the fascination for steam did not leave him, he was encouraged to engage his brain in a different direction.

The next thing to catch Henry's imagination was the workings of the watch. With his keen intellect and dogged persistence, he was soon dismantling and repairing all types of timepieces, making his own rudimentary tools. It is often said that this was the dawning of his entrepreneurial spirit. His workspace, a bench under his bedroom window, was soon busy with non-functioning watches that he would repair for a small fee.

At the age of 12, Henry's young life was about to be altered irrevocably. Not only was he given access to a portable steam engine that had recently arrived in the Dearborn area, which the owner Fred Reden allowed him to start and run, but he later also saw a steam engine travelling under its own power. The young, enquiring mind immediately needed to inspect and understand this, and any hope of him taking up the life of a farmer began to fade from his father's mind as he lost his son to the power and possibility of engineering.

This was also the year that Henry's beloved mother died. The woman who had touched and influenced his life so immensely was suddenly gone, and though he still had the love and support of his father and siblings, Henry was greatly impacted by her loss. He subsequently described the house as 'being like a watch without a mainspring'.

During the next few years on the farm, he became increasingly disenchanted with the life of a farmer and more influenced by the world of engineering and innovation. When Henry reached the age of 16, his father, always a fair and compassionate man, gave up on the idea of him becoming a third-generation farmer, and blessed his choice of becoming an engineer. To this end, Henry headed for Detroit and work in the Michigan Car Company Works, which made streetcars. William felt that Henry could do better and arranged an apprenticeship for him with James Flower and Bros Machine Shop to become a machinist. Eighteen months later he moved to the Detroit Dry Dock Company to study heavy industry.

In 1882 he carried all of his newly learnt expertise back with him to his father's farm, drawn not by the need to help his father however, but by the new steam traction engine purchased by one of William's neighbours. Henry was the natural choice to maintain and drive the engine, and showing his earlier entrepreneurial spirit, he was soon repairing these early Westinghouse engines in the surrounding area.

It was shortly after returning home that

ABOVE **Norman Rockwell painting of Henry and Clara Ford with a Quadricycle.** *(Ford Images)*

Henry Ford met Clara Bryant. After a three-year courtship (Clara's mother felt that, at 19, she was too young to marry in 1885), they finally married in 1888. Henry's father gave them a substantial plot of land, much of which was woodland. Henry immediately hired a portable steam engine with a circular saw. Using the plans for a house which the poised and modest Clara had drawn up, he cleared the land and began building it.

Two years later, Henry was offered a job at the Edison Electric Illuminating Company as a night operating engineer. The opportunity to gain knowledge of electrical engineering while working for Thomas Edison was hugely tempting, though the promised wage of $40 a month was fairly modest. Even though this meant renting a property in Detroit, Clara supported him. Their move was a success, with Henry being promoted to become the manager of the entire steam engine maintenance department (and incidentally almost doubling his salary) in little more than a year.

When their son Edsel was born in November

1893, they, as with most people, faced a hard winter. There was hardship everywhere, with little work and low pay. When Edsel was a few weeks old, one of the engines in Edison's main plant broke down, and Henry was called to repair the damage. Following this, his salary was increased at regular intervals.

Now, his ever-enquiring mind turned to thoughts of new kinds of propulsion until, in 1896, with Clara's constant belief and support, he eventually produced his first car, the Quadricycle. Subsequent events and the development of his cars are dealt with elsewhere in this book, but suffice to say Ford exhibited determination and doggedness as he strived to convince various backers to support his projects, eventually culminating in the formation of the Ford Motor Company.

This intuitive mechanic began to think along the lines of making the automobile more affordable, and therefore more available to the ordinary working man. To achieve this he would need to be able to design a basic car that could be produced at high levels for less money. Setting up a vast new factory where workers stood in one place, doing one job all day long, with the component parts coming to them on a moving assembly line was a massive stroke of innovation developed by himself and other engineers. This was indeed the dawn of mass production which was subsequently used for making televisions, fridges and countless other everyday items, and straddled the agricultural to the industrial era. This was the birth of Fordism, with Henry becoming almost a folk hero.

At this time Henry had a strong social conscience. He championed the working man having a car and of him being able to enjoy the resultant freedom to access more places and people. He used progressive methods with his employees, trying to encourage loyalty, stability and social wellbeing, increasing wages and shortening the working day. Encouraging clean living, sobriety and thrift was going perhaps a little beyond the remit of any employer, and could be construed as controlling and intrusive. As competition grew, this approach gave way to a much more authoritarian system using secret service men and spies to regulate the workforce. With his massive success came the need to control and dictate, and with these we see the first real signs of this quixotic genius morphing from idealist to autocrat.

However, in the early years, when he refused to pay the patent dues demanded by George B Selden (Selden had secured a patent on the automobile in 1895) he went against the consensus of opinion of the other car manufacturers, who all paid. He refused to pay (probably influenced as much by fiscal necessity as obduracy). For whatever reason, however, he stood up to Seldon who was trying to get his patent to cover all self-propelled wheeled vehicles built in the US, despite never having built one himself. Seldon and the other manufacturers then formed the Association of Licensed Automobile Manufacturers (ALAM) to try to control automotive competition but refused to let Ford join. Ford decided to fight the patent and, after eight years of wrangling through the courts, won his case. This is a great example perhaps of the occasional success of the arrogance of ignorance.

However, other parts of his belief system and nature were far more contentious. He was an avid anti-Semite. Nobody can say with any certainty from whence this hatred sprang, but on the purchase of *The Dearborn Independent* newspaper in 1919, he found the perfect vehicle for his venom. He used it as his mouthpiece against any form of Semitism – especially German Jewish bankers. Ford blamed the ills of the world on Jews, and once introduced to *The Protocols of the Elders of Zion*, which had in it a series of lectures purported to have been given by a Jewish elder on how to overthrow European governments, he became an avid, even rabid, anti-Semite. The paper was used for seven years to promote his feelings and beliefs, and was even given away free with every car that was sold. In 1927 Aaron Sapiro, a leading figure and activist in the farmers' cooperative movement, sued Ford for libel. Others had tried before, but Sapiro was the first to get a trial. Ford refused to testify, and settled out of court. After the debunking of *The Protocols of the Elders of Zion*, which was proved to be a total forgery, he was apparently devastated and even offered Jews his 'future friendship and goodwill', and in 1927 *The Dearborn Independent* was closed permanently. One has to wonder how this visionary could have had such distorted optics.

It certainly didn't escape the notice of the German Chancellor, Adolf Hitler, who was full of praise for Ford, and claimed to have kept a portrait of him by his desk. He also awarded him the Grand Cross of the German Eagle. Indeed, Ford was one of the few American companies that still dealt with Germany during the early war years, only ceasing in 1941 when America entered the war, and it became illegal for US motor companies to have any contact with their subsidiaries on German-controlled territory. It is reported that Ford's Dearborn facilities were completely cut off from their German plants after this point, but subsequently sued the US government for wartime damages to his German facilities due to Allied bombings. He was compensated to the tune of almost one million dollars.

Once America entered the war in 1941, Ford directed the building of a new factory near Detroit to produce B-24 bombers, and the first plane rolled off the line in 1942. At one point the plant was building 650 B-24s every month, eventually producing a staggering 8,865 of the bombers in total.

BELOW Henry Ford with his close friend Thomas Edison. *(Alamy)*

Another example of the strange dichotomies of this extraordinary man was that he was a devout pacifist in the First World War, sending his Peace Ship to Europe in 1915 in an attempt to convene a peace conference, but never flinched from letting force be used to encourage his workforce to 'toe the line'. Many years later, while refusing to acknowledge the United Auto Workers union, he used robust tactics to keep the unions under control. This was managed with violence and reprisals.

The problem was not going to go away, however. Edsel, who was a brilliant businessman, and who had recognised by the late '30s that this state of affairs could not continue, tried to push for collective bargaining as a process of negotiation. His father, who still held the final veto, refused to cooperate. Eventually his was the only automobile company not to recognise the UAW.

The last straw came for Henry in April 1941 when a sit-down strike was called by the union, and closed the River Rouge plant. Both distraught and furious, Henry Ford threatened to shut down his entire business. It must be remembered that this had been a tough and

dispiriting few years for him, and the man was well into his seventies, but apparently without the emotional equipment to let go. Also, Henry and Clara had for many years been true philanthropists who cared for their employees' welfare, and for the lot of the working man. He must have felt to a certain extent that he had bought and paid for his workforce's loyalty. This total chaos was only halted when the redoubtable Clara encouraged him to do right by his workers, and also ensure a future where their son and grandchildren could take over the Ford family business. With a total volte-face, the Ford Motor Company offered the most favourable terms by the time the contract was signed in June of 1941.

In 1913, Henry and Clara had drawn up plans for their astonishingly luxurious home which they named Fair Lane. It stood in 1,300 acres and by the time it was completed in December 1915, the luxury house and estate contained an indoor pool, stables, bowling alley, dance floor, skate barn, power house and staff accommodation. By the time they moved in, they had lived in 15 different homes.

Clara was a passionate and caring woman who supported and believed in her husband with absolute loyalty throughout their married life. She was not overawed by his mercurial rise, but stood equal to him. She often accompanied him on his business trips, and kept him calm and level. She stood strong through the moves to different homes, keeping both Henry and Edsel happy and secure. As the business grew exponentially, so did the couple's unwavering philanthropy. Clara was a great advocate of the suffrage movement, supporting amongst other things unwed mothers and helping women to gain skills in medical care. Both Clara and Henry were truly welfare capitalists. She made Fair Lane into a warm and loving haven for family and friends until her death in 1950.

In 1916, Ford, along with his close friends Thomas Edison, Harvey Firestone and John Burroughs decided to utilise the vehicles for leisure. To this end they loaded up with the basics and went camping in a truly back to nature style. The 'Vagabonds', as they titled themselves, employed their love of the land and lived as close to the earth as they could for a few weeks at a time. They

enjoyed companionship and a chance to clear their minds and truly relax. These happy and probably therapeutic escapes gradually changed shape and direction, with wives and friends wanting to join the party, with butlers, maids and cooks. After ten years, and perhaps due to their advancing years, and the exercise having lost its point and charm, these adventures were disbanded.

In 1923 Clara and Henry revived the dancing and music so beloved from their youth. They had met at a dance all of those years earlier, and both still loved to dance well into their advancing years.

Meanwhile, from the age of 11, Edsel had been going straight to the factory after school where he made himself useful running messages, stamping envelopes and generally doing the job of a clerk. He went straight into the Ford Company when he left school, and by 1919 was made president when his father suddenly stepped down from the position. He held the presidency for 25 years.

Edsel was a brilliant businessman and became the most outstanding industrialist of his generation. He was a visual communicator, and was a hugely skilled artist. Father and son in many ways made a perfect combination; Henry the genius engineer and Edsel with a real talent

for innovative design. The relationship between the two was not always harmonious, however, with Henry becoming increasingly unpredictable. There would often be fierce rows, usually instigated by Henry, who would not hesitate to denigrate his son when he felt the need. This often made Clara very angry with her husband.

Edsel was key in persuading his father to finally let go of the Model T and move on to other designs for motor vehicles. He was also hugely influential in the war effort, setting the goal of one B-24 being built every hour. Edsel developed stomach cancer and died aged 49 in 1943, leaving behind a wife and four children.

Henry resumed the role of president of the company for a short while, but stepped down in favour of his grandson Henry Ford II soon after the ending of the Second World War. During his final years he suffered several heart attacks and strokes, and finally succumbed to a cerebral haemorrhage in 1947 at the age of 83.

His progressive methods helped revolutionise manufacturing and enabled him to become a household name and also to become one of the richest men in the world. He opened up the opportunity for the ordinary working man to own a motor vehicle. He was a philanthropist who rewarded loyalty. He loved to dance. He gave us the Model T.

Chapter Two
Anatomy of a Model T

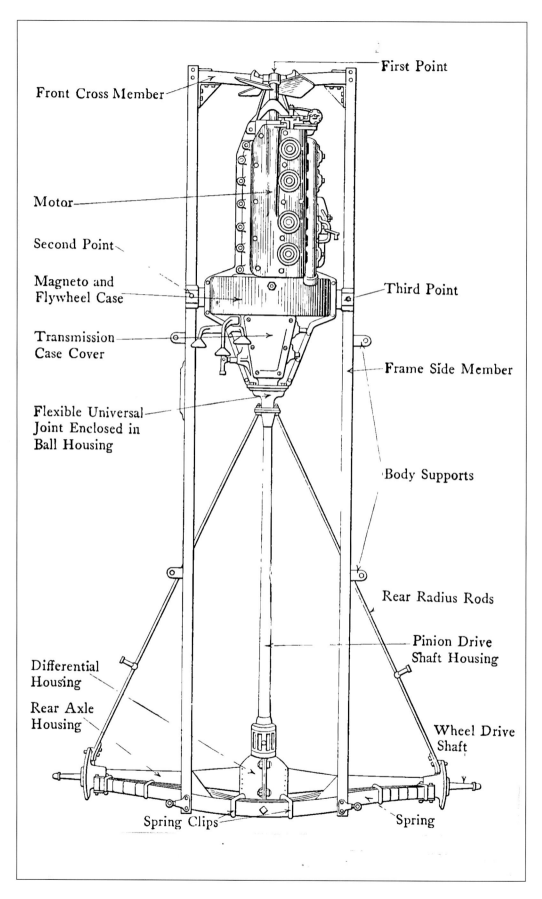

Front Cross Member

First Point

Motor

Second Point

Magneto and Flywheel Case

Third Point

Transmission Case Cover

Frame Side Member

Flexible Universal Joint Enclosed in Ball Housing

Body Supports

Rear Radius Rods

Pinion Drive Shaft Housing

Differential Housing

Rear Axle Housing

Wheel Drive Shaft

Spring Clips

Spring

LEFT **Original chassis rails at Tuckett Brothers works. The rails are constructed of channel-section pressed vanadium steel.** *(Author)*

The chassis

The chassis frame of a Model T Ford consists of two longitudinal side members, linked at each end by a curved cross member. The radiator, engine, scuttle and firewall are bolted directly to the chassis. The firewall is made of wood (until 1923 when it was replaced by steel) and positioned between the engine and the driving compartment. Running boards and fenders are attached at either side.

The side members, which are about 100in (2.5m) in length, are constructed of channel-section pressed vanadium steel. 'It's not that thick,' explains Neil Tuckett, 'and while vanadium steel cost a lot more to produce, Henry Ford was able to use about half the amount, so there was a slight gain and it made the chassis flexible.' Even so, after the first 2,500 models had been built, thicker steel was used for the frames. The original thickness of steel had proved to be too light and reinforcing plates had to be riveted inside the rails of the frame of those first 2,500 models.

The chassis of the Model TT, or Ton Truck, is 120in (3m) in length, rather than the 100in of the standard Model T, and the sections are much more substantial.

The corners of the chassis frame are braced by reinforcing brackets, riveted to the side and cross members.

The front cross member of the chassis curves down to support the transverse semi-elliptic spring, while the rear cross member curves upwards to match the rear transverse spring. The front axle is supported at three points by two spring shackles attached to the ends of the transverse leaf spring, and via two steel tubes that run in a V-shape back from these points to the bottom of the crankcase.

The engine is also attached at three points – at the front to the centre of the front cross member, and then further back on each side member. The front attachment is via a trunnion joint, which is

BELOW **The corners of the chassis frame are braced by reinforcing brackets.** *(Author)*

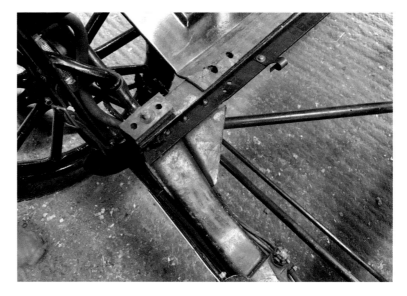

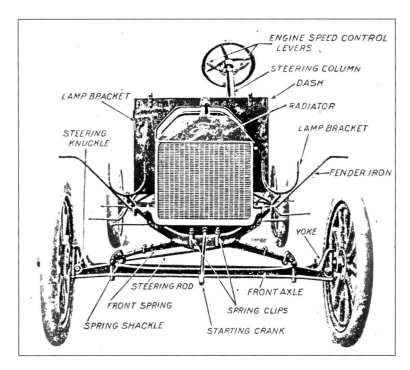

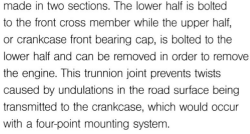

ENGINE SPEED CONTROL LEVERS

STEERING COLUMN

DASH

RADIATOR

LAMP BRACKET

FENDER IRON

LAMP BRACKET

STEERING KNUCKLE

YOKE

STEERING ROD

FRONT AXLE

FRONT SPRING

SPRING CLIPS

SPRING SHACKLE

STARTING CRANK

ABOVE Front view of chassis showing front axle and spring suspension. *(Pagé)*

RIGHT Lower half of trunnion joint, which forms the front engine mounting. *(Author)*

RIGHT A view towards the rear of the chassis, showing the large spherical bearing which joins the drive-shaft casing (torque tube) to the rear of the engine/transmission. The drive is taken to a universal joint by the square stub. *(Author)*

OPPOSITE The chassis of a very early two-lever Model T (see page 62). *(Alamy)*

made in two sections. The lower half is bolted to the front cross member while the upper half, or crankcase front bearing cap, is bolted to the lower half and can be removed in order to remove the engine. This trunnion joint prevents twists caused by undulations in the road surface being transmitted to the crankcase, which would occur with a four-point mounting system.

Pressed bracket supports for the body are attached to the side members, to which the body is bolted. The earlier Model Ts featured forged rear brackets to support the body and fenders, but from May 1913 a longer cross member eliminated the need for rear body brackets. From 1920 the forged running board brackets were replaced by pressings.

Chassis are used as the basis for dating Model T Fords, although until December 1925 they were not numbered. With the introduction of the 'Improved' Model Ts from the end of 1925, a number was stamped on the top right of the chassis, below the floorboards. Cars with a wooden firewall (pre-1923) may have a serial number plate attached to it.

The basic chassis of the Model T remained largely unaltered throughout its life, as Chris Barker, archivist of the Model T Ford Register of Great Britain, explains. 'There were tweaks to the rear cross member because the spring changed to adjust the ride height, and tweaks to the mudguard supports,' he says. 'But the basic frame, the front cross member, the engine and other supports, all stayed the same.'

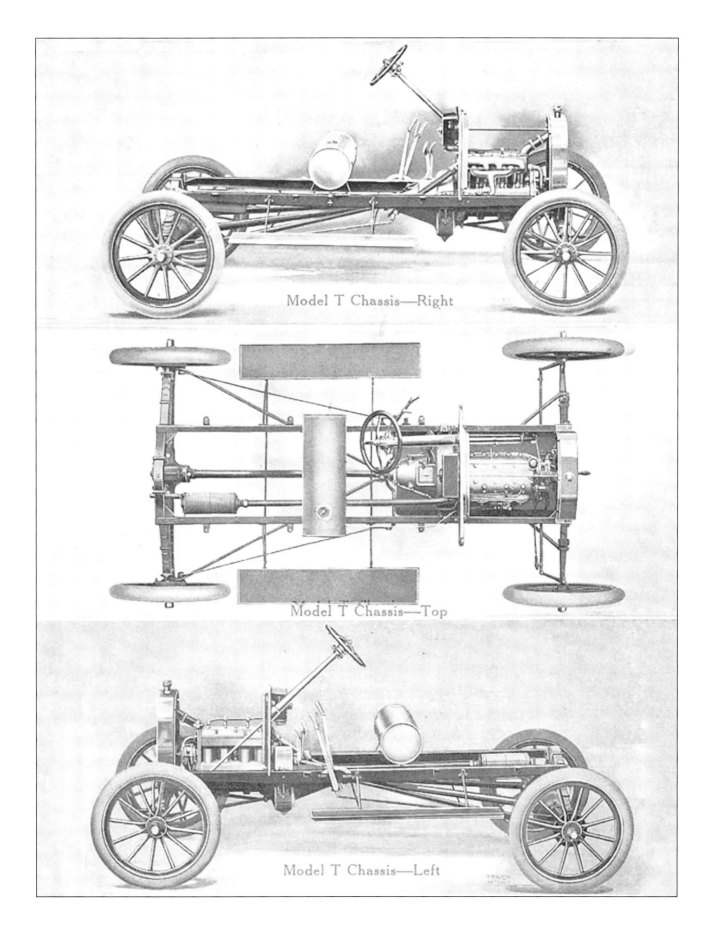

Model T Chassis—Right

Model T Chassis—Top

Model T Chassis—Left

Ford Model T. *(Getty Images)*

1 Hood
2 Throttle lever
3 Steering wheel
4 Spark lever
5 Dashboard
6 Horn
7 Radiator
8 Headlamp
9 Cooling fan
10 Transverse, semi-elliptic leaf spring
11 Starting handle
12 Front axle
13 12-spoke wooden wheel
14 Front radius rod
15 Exhaust manifold
16 Engine
17 Coil box
18 Brake pedal
19 Reverse pedal
20 Low-speed pedal
21 Transmission case
22 Battery
23 Running board
24 Rear radius rod
25 Propellor shaft within torque tube
26 Fuel tank
27 Rear axle
28 Exhaust box
29 Transverse leaf spring
30 Hub brake assembly

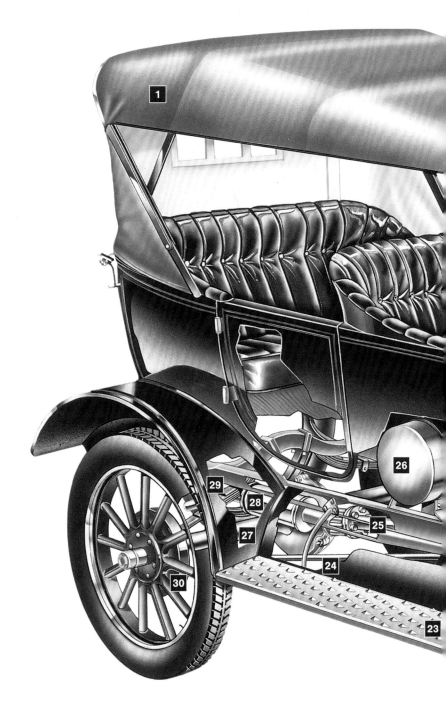

RIGHT One end of the transverse rear spring. *(Author)*

BELOW Rear view of the chassis showing rear suspension. *(Pagé)*

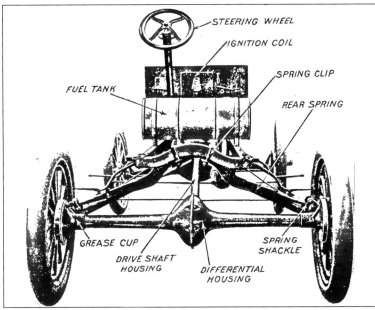

STEERING WHEEL

IGNITION COIL

SPRING CLIP

FUEL TANK

REAR SPRING

GREASE CUP

SPRING SHACKLE

DRIVE SHAFT HOUSING

DIFFERENTIAL HOUSING

as a torque tube, runs from the back of the transmission to the rear-axle casing.

The early rear axles were drawn and riveted, but proved to be fragile. 'There were various bits on the car that were too light, the most notable being the rear axle,' explains Chris Barker. 'This was a phenomenal achievement in terms of developing deep-drawn pressing technology; each of the two halves was a single pressing. They pressed the half-differential and the tube as one bit and they just bolted them together. That was a step too far, though. It was probably fine with a lightweight body on it, but by the time they put heavier bodies on it and owners found they could carry goods and started overloading it, they had to do something better.' As a result, cars soon had steel tubes fitted into cast differential casings.

Steering

The steering wheel of the Model T has four spokes that meet at a hub in the middle, beneath which is a planetary reduction gear system. This is an unusual feature since most cars of the time utilised a worm gear located at the bottom rather than the top of the steering column.

LEFT Steering wheel on an early Model T Ford with throttle and spark lever mounted underneath. Most Model T steering wheels were made of 'Fordite', an early plastic made from soya, while some early cars had wooden rims. *(Author)*

The steering wheel is connected by a very short shaft to a central sun gear. This meshes with three planetary gears that roll around an internal annular gear formed on the inside of the casing. The planets are on a three-stud carrier attached to the top of the steering column. At the bottom of the column, a 'Pitman arm' connects to a transverse link, the other end of which connects to the track rod.

It requires only one-and-a-quarter turns to go from lock-to-lock. 'It's a very basic, direct system that started as a 4:1 ratio,' says Neil Tuckett. 'When they put the bigger tyres on in the 1920s, it went to a 5.1 ratio.'

Brakes

There are two brakes on the Model T Ford – one acting on the transmission gear, the other acting on the drums of the rear wheels. The transmission, or service, brake is operated by the brake pedal. When this is pushed forward it tightens a fabric-lined brake band around the drum that forms the casing for the multiple clutch unit, to which the propeller shaft is attached. As the band tightens, it prevents the transmission, and hence the wheels, from turning and, if pushed firmly enough, will cause the car to come to a complete stop. Prior to 1925, the brake band was the same size as the other two bands in the transmission, but with the introduction of the 'Improved car' this was increased in width.

The other brake is operated by the hand lever to the side of the driving compartment. When the lever is pulled backwards it causes two semicircular cast-iron shoes located within the hub brake drum of each wheel to be pushed outwards against the pressed steel drum, stopping the movement of the wheels. The shoes are attached to spring coils which keep them in position away from the drum until the lever is pulled. Once the lever is released, the springs return the shoes to their normal position, allowing the wheel to rotate freely again.

The emergency brake lever is connected to the high gear clutch mechanism, so that when it is pulled by a certain amount the clutch will be disengaged but the brakes remain off until the lever is pulled back to its full extent. It can also be locked in any desired position by a ratchet and pawl mechanism.

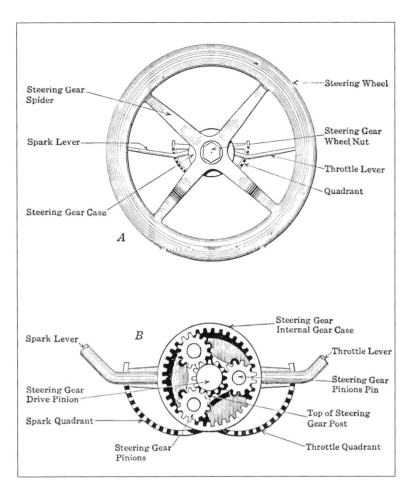

ABOVE Diagram of the steering wheel with throttle and spark levers (A) and planetary reduction gearing (B). *(Pagé)*

BELOW The track rod connects to the upright on which the wheel is mounted. *(Author)*

RIGHT **Diagram of**
rear axle with wheel
removed to show
workings of brake.
(Pagé)

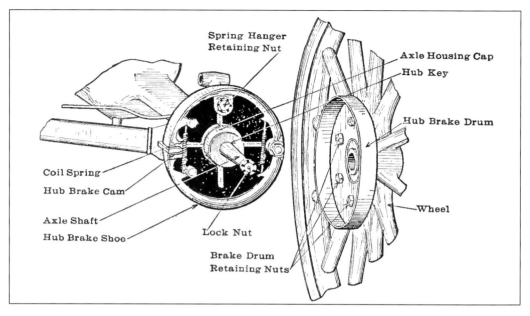

'The brakes are interesting, put it that way,' says Neil Tuckett. 'They are limited and there are many ways of braking. The biggest brake is your engine – shut it down – followed by the footbrake, which is on the transmission. That's OK, but it's oil-immersed. You've got a handbrake, which you can yank on in an emergency, that acts on the rear brakes. The rear shoes later became bigger and more efficient. You can also brake using reverse gear and you can brake by using first gear.

'So you can use any combination of those, and they all add up to being "adequate". Many people today will bolt on what they call a Rocky Mountain brake kit, which is additional brakes on the footbrake, putting a bigger external band on the rear drum. On the earlier cars, 1925 or earlier, with an 8in (20cm) drum you put an additional bigger drum on, but on the 1926–27 cars, which already have a bigger drum, you put a band around the outside. Purely for modern traffic, they're a good idea. You can even buy disc brakes today and put them on, but I think that's going a step too far with a hundred-year-old vehicle. They're very efficient, but it's still down to two bits of rubber on the road, and two-wheel braking, not four-wheel braking.

'I had an interesting conundrum,' he adds. 'I sent a car out to Italy but the authorities there won't register it because it hasn't got four-wheel brakes. The owner is now trying to put four-wheel brakes on to it to keep the Italian authorities at bay because he wants to use it on the road.'

The engine

The Ford engine is a 2.9-litre (177-cu in) straight four-cylinder, with the cylinders cast in a single iron block, integral with the top half of the crankcase. The engine was designed to be easy to repair and features one intake and exhaust valve per cylinder, produces 20hp, to give a top speed of 40–45mph (64–72kph), and can run on gasoline (petrol), sometimes mixed with kerosene, or ethanol. These fuels were in common use in rural areas of America;

ABOVE AND ABOVE RIGHT The Ford engine in the 1926 'Improved' Coupé. Note the coil box is mounted on top of the engine, rather than on the dashboard (as in earlier models), and the 'vaporizer' carburettor which heats the fuel. *(Author)*

RIGHT Top view of the Ford engine showing the removeable cylinder head, allowing access to the combustion chambers, valves and pistons. *(Pagé)*

kerosene was widely used in farm tractors and stationary engines, while ethanol was a home-produced alcohol which was popular as a fuel until Prohibition in 1919 prevented its use.

The bore of the cylinders is 3¾in (95mm) and the stroke 4in (102mm). All the valves are on one side of the engine in what is known as an 'L' configuration and the camshaft spins at half the speed of the crankshaft.

Four main types of engine block exist. From 1908–11, the valves were open and the first 2,500 cars were fitted with a water pump. From 1911–22 the valves had two-piece covers fitted, with a one-piece cover from 1922 onwards. From 1919–27 the block and timing cover had provision for a generator to be mounted on the right-hand side, while from 1925–27, the block incorporated a pair of cast lugs on the back face near the top, with tapped holes, in order to allow the transmission cover, or 'hog's head', to be bolted on (information taken from *The Essential Buyer's Guide: Ford Model T* by Chris Barker and Neil Tuckett).

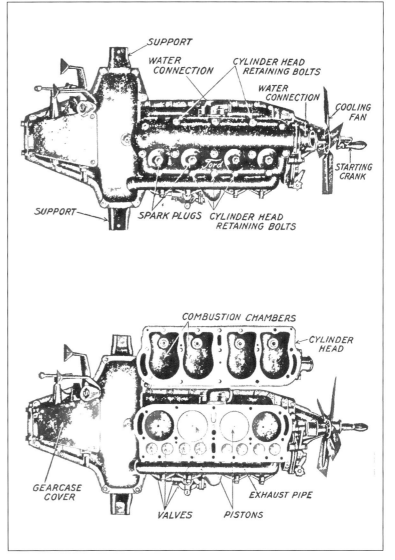

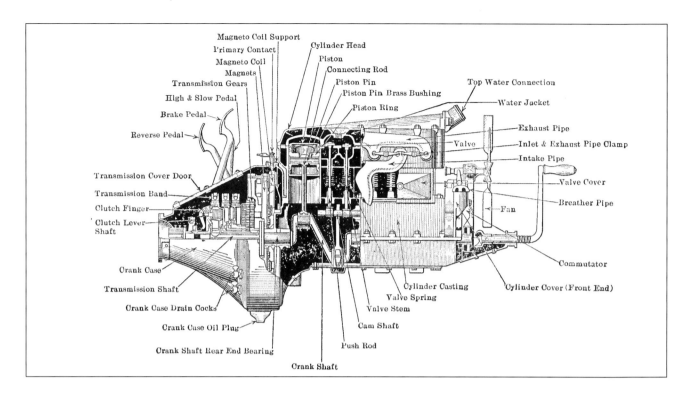

Labels on the sectional view of the Ford engine:

Magneto Coil Support
Primary Contact
Magneto Coil
Magnets
Transmission Gears
High & Slow Pedal
Brake Pedal
Reverse Pedal

Cylinder Head
Piston
Connecting Rod
Piston Pin
Piston Pin Brass Bushing
Piston Ring

Top Water Connection
Water Jacket
Exhaust Pipe
Valve
Inlet & Exhaust Pipe Clamp
Intake Pipe
Valve Cover
Breather Pipe
Fan

Transmission Cover Door
Transmission Band
Clutch Finger
Clutch Lever Shaft

Crank Case
Transmission Shaft
Crank Case Drain Cocks
Crank Case Oil Plug
Crank Shaft Rear End Bearing
Crank Shaft

Cylinder Casting
Valve Spring
Valve Stem
Cam Shaft
Push Rod

Commutator
Cylinder Cover (Front End)

ABOVE Sectional view of the Ford engine.
(Pagé)

The cylinder head, of which two variations exist, is cast iron. The 'low' head was in use until late 1916 when it was succeeded by the 'high' head, which had a higher top face to allow more volume for water. The high head has a lower compression ratio than the low head (4:1 as opposed to 4.5:1) and therefore produces slightly less power.

Connecting rods are made from vanadium steel and the crankshaft is a vanadium steel forging, supported by three main bearings: one at each end and one in the centre. A pressed steel plate covers the bottom of the crankcase, and the big-end bearings can be accessed by removing this steel cover. Unlike the chassis, all engines are numbered.

The engine is mounted to the chassis frame at only three points: one on each side at the rear and a single, flexible mounting on the front cross member. This comprises a cylindrical bearing in a trunnion. As explained on page 41 in the section about the chassis, the trunnion joint is in two sections, the upper section being removeable to allow the engine to be taken out, while the trunnion joint itself means that twists in the chassis frame caused by uneven road surfaces would not be transferred to the engine.

Cooling

The first 2,447 engines produced featured water pumps, but later models use thermosyphon action to circulate the water. This operates on the principle that hot water is less dense than cold and so rises as it heats up to circulate the coolant in the system. The top of the water jacket around the cylinder head is connected to the top of the radiator, while a pipe from the bottom of the radiator connects to a manifold at the bottom of the cylinder block.

For the system to work, the radiator has to be high enough for the water to flow into

BELOW The Ford thermosyphon system.
(Pagé)

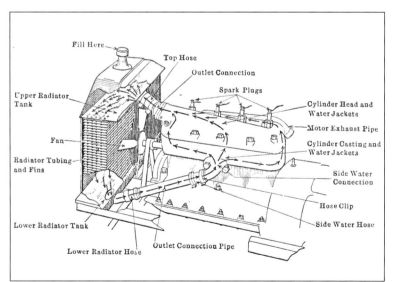

Labels on the thermosyphon system:

Fill Here
Top Hose
Outlet Connection
Spark Plugs
Cylinder Head and Water Jackets
Motor Exhaust Pipe
Cylinder Casting and Water Jackets
Side Water Connection
Hose Clip
Side Water Hose
Outlet Connection Pipe
Lower Radiator Hose
Lower Radiator Tank
Radiator Tubing and Fins
Fan
Upper Radiator Tank

the bottom of the water jacket by gravity. As it becomes heated, it rises to the top of the jacket surrounding the cylinders and then into the radiator where it is cooled, falling to the bottom to begin recirculating again.

Ignition

The ignition system uses a low-voltage magneto (actually an alternator) incorporated in the flywheel, to which 16 permanent magnets are attached; the flywheel housing providing protection from water. A fixed plate attached to the back of the engine block contains 16 corresponding coils so that when the engine is running, the magnets attached to the flywheel pass the coils, creating a low-voltage alternating current. This passes to a coil box mounted on the dashboard (on the engine from 1925), containing four trembler coils which are connected to a four-contact timer mounted at the front of the camshaft, and also to the four

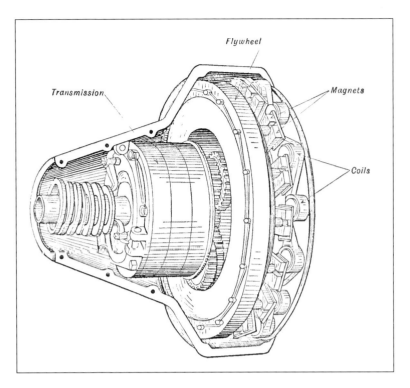

ABOVE Diagram showing the coils and magnets that make up the Ford magneto, along with the flywheel and transmission gear. *(Pagé)*

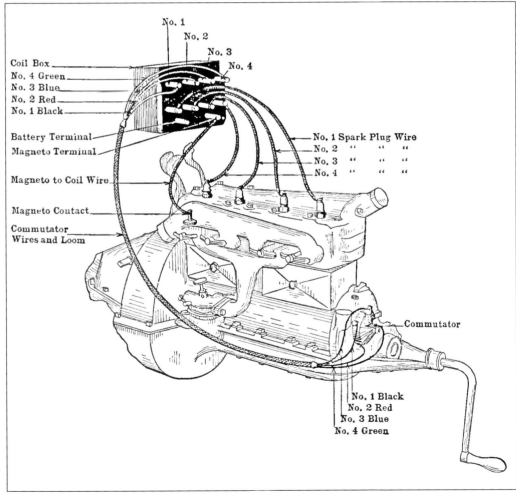

LEFT The Ford ignition system. *(Pagé)*

RIGHT **The flywheel with its sixteen magnets.** *(Author)*

spark plugs in the engine, the firing sequence of which is 1, 2, 4, 3.

'The magneto was a development that Henry Ford introduced,' commented Neil Tuckett. 'One of his men was a good electrician who worked it out.'

A single master vibrator was offered as an aftermarket accessory but not deemed necessary as the four separate trembler coils rarely proved problematic and are fairly easy to adjust.

Prior to December 1918, a starter motor was not fitted since hand-cranking using the starter handle generated enough current to start the engine. Hand-cranking was a familiar practice in rural America. The low compression ratio of the engine makes it relatively easy to crank and the low-voltage magneto supplies an adequate current at low revolutions. As a result, the Model T was supplied without a battery.

'That's how mean Ford was,' laughed Neil Tuckett. 'Early on, he gave you a position to connect a battery, but you had to go and buy one after you'd bought the car. He expected you to swing it and start it on the Ford magneto, which is not the easiest thing to do if it's not in perfect condition.' However, Chris Barker commented:

RIGHT AND FAR RIGHT **Neil Tuckett demonstrates how the fixed plate, to which the sixteen coils of the magneto are attached, fits to the flywheel with its corresponding 16 magnets.** *(Author)*

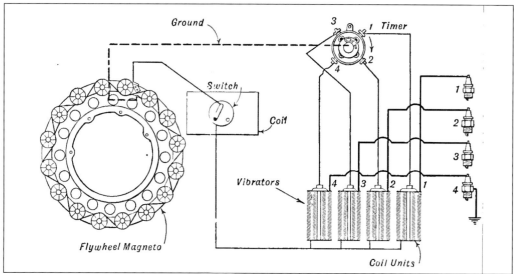

RIGHT **Wiring diagram for Ford ignition system.** *(Pagé)*

'Henry Ford's motives for the magneto system and no battery were that he didn't want the owner to be dependent on having a good charged battery to be able to run the car.'

From December 1918 onwards, a starter motor and generator were fitted, the latter requiring a modification to the block in order to accommodate it, and from then on a battery was supplied as standard.

Lubrication

A novel form of splash lubrication is used. The magnets of the dynamo attached to the flywheel dip into the oil as the flywheel rotates and fling it upwards to be caught in a small trough. An internal pipe carries it forward by gravity to the timing gears. The oil then flows back under the big-end bearings.

'The engine is a basic three-litre, side valve engine, completely restricted by the amount of air and fuel you can get in,' said Neil Tuckett. 'It only revs to 1,900rpm and maximum power is at about 1,600 [maximum torque at 1,000], so it's a very basic diesel-like engine, but it pulls from 300 revs so is very torquey. It's very simple and there's very little to go wrong. The only Achilles heel is probably the crankshaft. It's a bent bit of wire and it's not unknown for them to break. Certainly, they were breaking in period, but if they were producing 8,000 a day, and they were drop-forging them, there were going to be faults there. If we have a crank out now we crack-test it and nine times out of ten it will still be ok.'

Fuel supply

Fuel is carried in a galvanised iron tank which holds 10 US gallons (38 litres), located beneath the front seat, and conveyed to the float-feed-type carburettor via a soft copper tube. The fuel enters the carburettor, is vaporised and passes through an inlet pipe into the combustion chamber. A hot air pipe feeds air from around the exhaust pipe to the carburettor to aid vaporising of the fuel.

The carburettor can be adjusted using the needle valve, which regulates the flow of fuel. An adjusting rod is located within the driving compartment for use during cold weather starting.

Because the fuel is fed into the engine by gravity, problems could sometimes arise when

ABOVE Engine-mounted coil box on 1926 'Improved' Coupé with cover removed. *(Author)*

BELOW The Ford Model T fuel system. *(Pagé)*

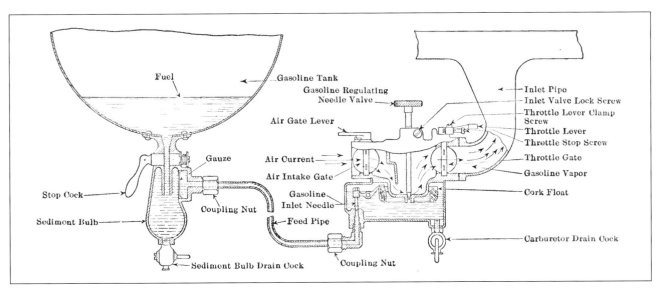

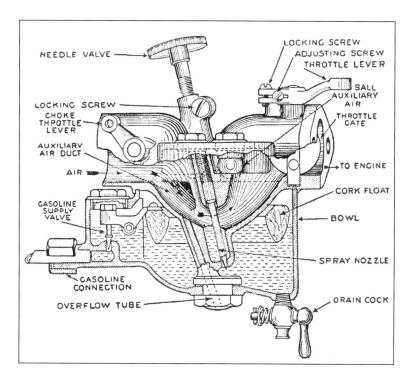

NEEDLE VALVE

LOCKING SCREW
ADJUSTING SCREW
THROTTLE LEVER

BALL
AUXILIARY
AIR

THROTTLE
GATE

TO ENGINE

CORK FLOAT

BOWL

SPRAY NOZZLE

DRAIN COCK

LOCKING SCREW
CHOKE
THROTTLE
LEVER

AUXILIARY
AIR DUCT

AIR

GASOLINE
SUPPLY
VALVE

GASOLINE
CONNECTION

OVERFLOW TUBE

ABOVE **A sectioned view of the special Kingston carburettor used on some Model Ts. Note the cork float, and the adjustable needle valve. The more common carburettor used was the Holley NH.** *(Pagé)*

BELOW **Plan view of the planetary gearing and clutch assembly.** *(Pagé)*

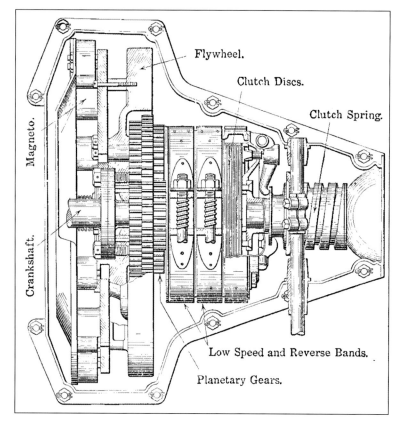

Flywheel.

Clutch Discs.

Clutch Spring.

Magneto.

Crankshaft.

Low Speed and Reverse Bands.

Planetary Gears.

driving up a steep hill – the engine being starved of fuel. The solution was to reverse up.

'Improved' (post August 1925) cars had the tank located higher in the scuttle, which solved the hill-climb problem. These cars also had a 'Vaporizer' carburettor which heated the fuel – introduced to cope with poor fuel quality in the USA.

Transmission

Henry Ford was conscious that not many people at the time knew how to drive and that those who did often found a straight-cut sliding gear system (long before the days of synchromesh) difficult to master. The answer was an ingenious two-speed plus reverse system which utilises planetary (or epicyclic) gears that are constantly in mesh.

The system consists of three drums which, when the car is running in high gear, are all locked and spin around together, taking the drive to the back axle via a wet multiplate clutch. Surrounding each drum is a band which, when a pedal is pushed, will lock that particular drum, preventing it from rotating. This causes one set of the planetary gears to revolve around it, taking the drive, at the same time releasing the multiplate clutch. Depending on which pedal is pressed, this will either select slow gear, reverse or brake the rear axle completely.

According to Neil Tuckett, the system was very advanced for its time, but was all known Victorian technology. 'The idea had come from the end of drivelines in factories,' he explains, 'where you had a long driveline driving all the machinery, and you had a couple of pulleys on the drivelines. You'd have a motor, or water or whatever, driving the belts and you'd move the belt across from one pulley to another. So you either had a direct drive or if you moved the belt to the other pulley, you could have a different ratio.

'In addition to that, you had another pulley, so you'd normally have three, and that was the idle pulley, so if you went right across to that your driveline stopped. So you had stop, slow and fast, just by moving a belt. And that's where the phrases "knock-on" and "knock-off" come from. When it was the old boys' tea time, they'd get a wooden stick and knock the drive off.

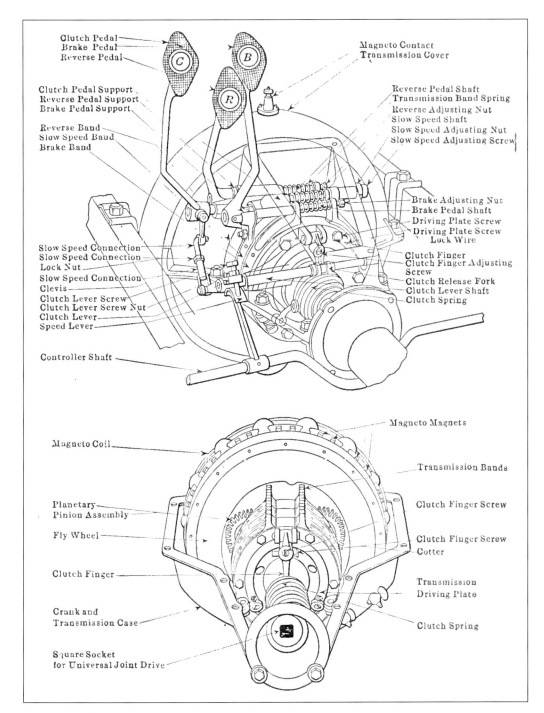

Clutch Pedal
Brake Pedal
Reverse Pedal

Clutch Pedal Support
Reverse Pedal Support
Brake Pedal Support

Reverse Band
Slow Speed Band
Brake Band

Magneto Contact
Transmission Cover

Reverse Pedal Shaft
Transmission Band Spring
Reverse Adjusting Nut
Slow Speed Shaft
Slow Speed Adjusting Nut
Slow Speed Adjusting Screw

Brake Adjusting Nut
Brake Pedal Shaft
Driving Plate Screw
Driving Plate Screw
Lock Wire

Clutch Finger
Clutch Finger Adjusting Screw
Clutch Release Fork
Clutch Lever Shaft
Clutch Spring

Slow Speed Connection
Slow Speed Connection
Lock Nut
Slow Speed Connection
Clevis
Clutch Lever Screw
Clutch Lever Screw Nut
Clutch Lever
Speed Lever

Controller Shaft

Magneto Coil

Magneto Magnets

Transmission Bands

Clutch Finger Screw

Planetary
Pinion Assembly

Fly Wheel

Clutch Finger

Crank and
Transmission Case

Square Socket
for Universal Joint Drive

Clutch Finger Screw Screw
Cotter

Transmission
Driving Plate

Clutch Spring

'Henry Ford took that technology and put it behind his flywheel. Instead of moving a belt, you clamp a band to lock a drum. It's very simple. They developed the epicyclic transmission so it went through a set of triple gears to give a lower ratio. That was all Victorian technology but it's the basis for all modern automatics, since the clutch plate system and the epicyclic gears is how automatics operate today, albeit hydraulically.

'The real key to it is that the drums are only used for first and reverse gear. In top gear, it's all locked up and the crankshaft and all the transmission and prop shaft are turning as a mass at the same speed as the pinion at the back end, straight to the back axle. So there's nothing wearing in that gearbox at all.

'When you press a pedal with your foot, you are locking one of the three drums with a band, and by locking a drum you're introducing a

RIGHT AND FAR RIGHT The flywheel with planetary gears and transmission bands. *(Author)*

RIGHT Chris Barker demonstrates the position of the 25 clutch plates. *(Author)*

FAR RIGHT The clutch assembly in place. *(Author)*

drive through the epicyclic gears. That causes the reduction in the same way as the end of a driveline in a factory. So you have reverse going one way, first the other way, and then the brake which locks everything up, straight onto the prop shaft.'

The transmission is bolted directly to the back of the flywheel. Behind the engine block is the stator plate, which contains the coils of the magneto. Attached to that are three lateral pins that carry the three planetary pinions of the epicyclic system. Behind that sits the low and reverse speed drums, and the clutch assembly.

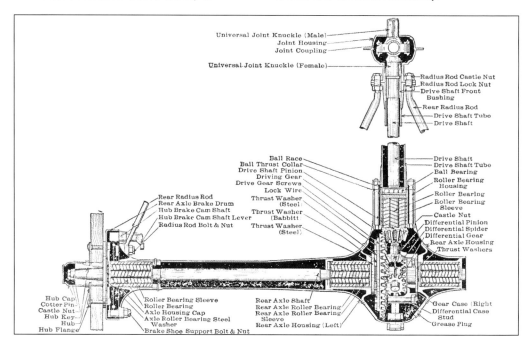

RIGHT Sectional view of the rear axle. *(Pagé)*

Drive from the gearbox is taken to the differential on the rear axle via a universal joint and thin propeller shaft, which is enclosed within a torque tube that serves to locate the rear axle and resist its tendency to rotate, caused by the transverse leaf springs not providing forward and backward support. The drive shaft is supported at the universal joint end by a plain bearing, while at the pinion end a large flexible roller bearing and a ball thrust bearing are used.

'In the rear of the transmission are 25 clutch plates which are clamped together by a big spring,' continues Neil Tuckett. 'When the spring is acting it's locking all that up. When you release the spring, they are able to spin freely amongst each other. That leads to the unique feature of the Model T having to be jacked up in the mornings to start it. On a cold day, you jack up a back wheel, because if there are 25 clutch plates and you've got sticky oil, it wants to drive. And if you start it with the crank handle – assuming you can start it with the sticky oil – quite often it'll pin you against the wall because it'll creep forward until it stops.

'So you jack up one rear wheel and that wheel spins like a flywheel. And that makes it easier to start. Once you've got it warm you can then free the clutch plates up.'

The transmission cover, which is known as a 'hog's head', was initially made from

LEFT One rear wheel jacked up to allow it to spin and aid starting. *(Author)*

aluminium, but from late 1915 onwards, this was replaced by iron. A removeable panel on the top allows access to the transmission bands. With the introduction of the starter motor in 1919, modifications were made to the 'hog's head' in order to accommodate the starter motor, and a ring gear was added to the flywheel. Otherwise the engine and transmission remained basically the same throughout the life of the Model T Ford.

With the introduction of the 'Improved' car in 1925, the brake band in the transmission was increased in width. Prior to this, all three bands had been identical.

Model TT

The rear axle of the Model TT, or Ton Truck, incorporates a worm drive and wheel, rather than the bevel gear and pinion of the car.

BELOW Details of the Ruckstell rear axle. The parts page comes from Ford's own parts book as the Ruckstell was the only approved accessory from an outside supplier, and is still available today. *(Chris Barker collection)*

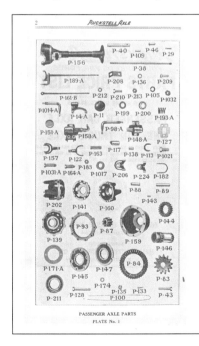

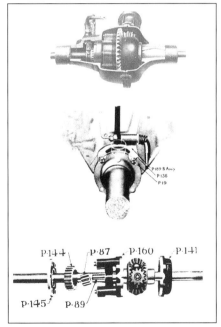

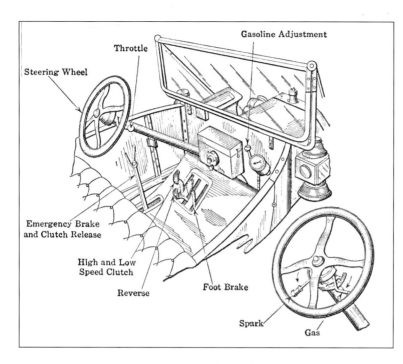

Diagram labels:
- Steering Wheel
- Throttle
- Gasoline Adjustment
- Emergency Brake and Clutch Release
- High and Low Speed Clutch
- Reverse
- Foot Brake
- Spark
- Gas

ABOVE Diagram of the driving compartment of a Model T Ford. *(Pagé)*

The worm is located at the end of the drive shaft, above the crown wheel. An aftermarket accessory, such as a Ruckstell twin-speed rear axle or Jumbo gearbox, which provided intermediate gears between low and high, was often added and was available for both trucks and cars.

RIGHT Driving compartment of a left-hand-drive 1926 'Improved' Model T Coupé. *(Author)*

RIGHT Handbrake lever and three pedals mounted on the floor. *(Author)*

FAR RIGHT Steering wheel with throttle control mounted underneath. *(Author)*

'If a gearbox is used, you can select neutral, so you must have Rocky Mountain brakes, which are additional brakes, on the rear,' cautions Neil Tuckett. 'With a Ruckstell rear axle you cannot get neutral, whereas a gearbox can, so if you put your footbrake on, nothing happens – there's no braking to the rear – so they have to be linked to additional Rocky Mountain brakes.' (See page 49 – Brakes.)

Driving compartment and instruments

The driving compartment of a Model T Ford is quite spartan, there being just the steering wheel, with its spark advance-retard and throttle levers, the handbrake lever and three pedals on the floor. There is only a single instrument, a speedometer, and not even a fuel gauge. After 1914, the speedometer was discontinued, becoming either an extra or an accessory. Prior to 1925 the coil box was mounted on the dashboard but on the later 'Improved' models it moved to the top of the engine.

Wooden planks fit on ledges along the inside of the body, the toe-board planks being angled to form a floor between the firewall and the seats.

'By 1914, Ford's production was such that he was outstripping the production of the Stewart Speedometer Company, which produced speedos,' explains Neil Tuckett. 'So Ford said, "Fine, five dollars off every car and buy it afterwards." He didn't put speedos back on until the Model A came along; you bought your own.

'When electrics came out, and by that I mean a starter motor and dynamo in late 1918, then Ford gave you an ammeter to show your charging system. Prior to that, there were no instruments at all. Ford gave you nothing, no accessories, you bought everything afterwards. He wouldn't have even given you mirrors.'

The layout of the pedals remained the same, regardless of whether the car was left- or right-hand drive. The left pedal is for changing between low and high gear, with low selected by pressing your foot down on the pedal. When the pedal is released, high gear is selected, while the halfway position selects neutral. The middle pedal, when pressed down, selects reverse gear and it is quite possible to do this while driving along, causing the car to slowly come to a halt and then start going backwards. The right pedal controls the transmission brake, which locks a band around the drum, preventing the transmission drum, and hence the wheels, from turning.

Oddly enough, the two steering-wheel-mounted levers did swap from side to side, depending on whether the car was left- or right-hand drive. 'The advance-retard is always on the outside, and the throttle always on the inside,' explains Neil Tuckett. 'The steering wheel moved from side to side but the levers swapped round. In the UK, once the starter motor and the dynamo appeared, they couldn't get the steering column down the side of the dynamo, so Ford decreed everything in the UK would be left-hand drive, and for three years, until January 1923, he only produced left-hand-drive cars. His idea, in my opinion, was to persuade the UK to change to left-hand drive. However, there were clever guys who decided to build kits, so you linked up the left-hand pedals and you made it right-hand drive, because some people didn't want to play.

'To be fair, if Ford had got away with it, the colonies and the Empire would have done the same and today the world would be left-hand drive pretty well throughout. He had the right idea but the British were stubborn and didn't do it.

'In Canada, [which was supplying RHD territories in the British Empire] they developed a different timing cover to have the dynamo belt-driven externally and then by 1923 redesigned the steering column bracket to accommodate the dynamo conventionally on right-hand-drive cars. Ford was obviously hell-bent on trying to

ABOVE Coil box mounted on the dashboard of a 1911 RHD Model T Tourer. *(Author)*

LEFT Switch on coil box is set to 'Magneto' or 'Battery', if the latter is fitted. *(Author)*

LEFT Speedometer on 1911 RHD Model T Tourer. *(Author)*

BELOW **The acetylene
generator for the
headlamps is mounted
on the running board
on the driver's side.**
(Author)

make us go left-hand drive but it was obvious we weren't going to switch, though we could have done.'

Prior to 1925, all three pedals were quite narrow, but with the introduction of the 'Improved' car the left- and right-hand pedals (low gear and brake) were increased in width.

On Fords built before 1914, when electric headlamps were introduced, on the outside of the driver's side of the compartment is the adjustment for the acetylene lighting. This is a knob on the top of the acetylene generator, which is located on the running board. The acetylene is produced by dripping water from a variable tap onto calcium carbide and it is the driver's job to control the flow of the water to adjust the brightness of the lights. (See page 71.)

When six-volt batteries became available, from around 1918, Ford provided a cradle under the back floorboards to accommodate them.

Bodywork

From the outset, the Model T Ford was offered in a range of body styles with usually two or four seats, and either open or closed and with or without doors. These included two-seater Coupés and Runabouts, two-seater Roadsters, four- (or, at a push, five-) seater Touring cars, six-seater Town cars and Landaulettes, where the rear-seat passengers are covered by a convertible top. All models were built on the same 100in (2.5m) chassis

**BELOW With the
floorboards removed,
the 'hogs head' cover
of the transmission can
be seen, and warm air
from the exhaust can
provide a rudimentary
form of heating.**
(Author)

EARLY TWO-LEVER MODELS

Very early Model Ts (between only 500 and 800 examples) had two levers, instead of one, and only two pedals, rather than three.

One lever purely operated the parking brakes, whereas the second lever selected high gear when pushed forward, neutral when halfway or straight up, and reverse when pulled hard back. The latter technique is tricky, since it can be awkward to get good enough leverage in order to keep reverse engaged.

The two pedals are for low gear and brake and perform the same operation as on any other Model T (low–neutral–high and brake).

and the available bodies evolved over the 19-year life of the car.

Windscreens were optional on the 1909 open cars, but were standard from 1910 onwards.

Selection of body styles

'The original car was tall and gawky and certainly of its time,' says Chris Barker. 'By the 1920s it had got lower and a little bit sleeker with special-bodied cars. The "T" was a middle-class car at first and later was good as a taxi.

'There was what they called the Touring Car, which was the four-seat open version,'

CONTINUED ON PAGE 66

1915 Ford Model T Tourer *(Richard Rimmer collection)*

1914 Ford Model T Roadster *(Richard Rimmer collection)*

1922 Ford Model T Centredoor *(Richard Rimmer collection)*

Ford Model T Tourabout *(Getty Images)*

Ford Model T Town car *(Wikimedia Commons)*

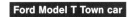

1914 Ford Model T Torpedo Runabout *(Neil Tuckett Collection)*

1920 Ford Model T Landaulette Taxi *(Alamy)*

1923 Ford Model T Tudor (two-door) *(Richard Rimmer collection)*

1924 Ford Model T Fordor (four-door) *(Richard Rimmer collection)*

1925 Ford Model T Speedster *(Richard Rimmer collection)*

1914 Ford Model T Tourer *(Richard Rimmer collection)*

1926 Ford Model T Tourer *(Neil Tuckett collection)*

1927 Ford Model T Coupé *(Richard Rimmer collection)*

1914 Ford Model T Roadster   *(Neil Tuckett collection)*

1911 Two-seater with Mother-in-law seat   *(Neil Tuckett collection)*

1921 Ford Model T Cabriolet   *(Neil Tuckett collection)*

1916 Ford Model T Coupelet *(Ford Images)*

he continues, 'while the Torpedo was a two-seater with a lower steering column. The Town car was a Landaulette with a separate rear compartment, and was the first closed Model T, designed for those with chauffeurs, while the Roadster was a two-seater. The Centredoor had two doors and the driver had to climb round or over. Then there were the two- and four-door Saloons and the Coupé, which is the closed two-seater version. The Coupelet is a sort of Coupé with a more sophisticated fold-down roof.

'Next, there were special-bodied trucks or vans, commercials based on Model T Ford car chassis, including the delivery van, which was mostly UK only, the ambulance, and then the Ton Truck as a van or drop-side lorry.

'They weren't all produced throughout the life of

1918 Light Van *(Richard Rimmer collection)*

the Model T,' he adds. 'The Tourer was produced all the way through, as was the two-seater, but the Landaulette was only made until 1922, while the Centredoor Sedan was 1916–24.'

'Ford had a very set group of body styles that he continued pretty well throughout,' adds Neil Tuckett, 'but small changes were happening every day. Originally one part might have had four rivets, but if he could save a rivet, and that was worth a cent, if you're producing 10,000 cars a day, a cent became a hundred dollars. Now a hundred dollars would pay for a man's wages for a month. That's the scale of the operation.'

In the UK, about 13% of cars and 50% of Ton Trucks were sold as just rolling chassis and were bodied by independent coachbuilders.

Painting

As explained in Chapter One, contrary to popular opinion, Model T Fords were available in colours other than just black, including grey, red and green, although black was the only option between 1914 and 1925.

During the painting process, the unpainted bodies were first given a coat of primer, followed by two coats of colour; each coat requiring 24 hours drying time in between. A moving line then conveyed them to where seats and upholstery were fitted and a final coat of clear varnish was applied.

'The paint was sprayed onto the body using an inch hose, like a compressor hose, with a watering can rose on the end,' explains Neil Tuckett. 'They used to hand-spray it and anything that wasn't caught with the spray was hand-finished. The waste paint used to go into a trough under the conveyor and back into the paint system. It was really that simple. Later on they were using proper spray guns and heat booths in the 1920s.

'In 1925 with the introduction of the "Improved" car, colours returned and they started to make the bodies a little more aerodynamic, with a few more curves than the early versions. The early ones had flat wings and then you go to the curved wings, and it was very much like a Model A at that point.'

Commercial vehicles

Commercial bodies for the Model T fell into two general categories: the Delivery Van, with panel (enclosed) bodies, and the Flatbed Truck, both with either open-sided or closed cabs.

1916 Van *(Richard Rimmer collection)*

1927 Truck *(Richard Rimmer collection)*

1923 Tipper Truck *(Richard Rimmer collection)*

1923 Charabanc *(Richard Rimmer collection)*

1923 English Van *(Neil Tuckett collection)*

1912 Pie Van *(Neil Tuckett collection)*

'From 1914 Ford UK supplied the first mass-produced van,' explains Chris Barker, 'which was unique to the UK but very successful. The Ton Truck appeared from 1917, first as just a chassis and cab, then with open and van bodywork. Trucks and vans allowed Ford UK to survive after 1921 when road tax was increased to £1 per RAC horsepower on cars. The annual tax on the Model T increased from £6, 6s to £23 (approx. £1,150 today), whereas a Morris Cowley was £12. UK Model T production peaked at 40,000 in 1920, with half being cars and half commercial vehicles. Commercial sales stayed up after 1921 because they were taxed differently; cars fell and Morris took the lead.'

'The two-seat pickups were available in the USA from late 1925 onwards,' adds Neil Tuckett, 'but they weren't available in the UK for some reason.'

More details of the Ton Truck can be found in Chapter Seven – Endless Varieties.

Ancillaries

Radiator

The radiator core is made from 95 copper tubes that pass through holes in 74 thin strips of brass. Using a specially designed machine, the tubes and brass strips could be slid together in a single operation and a radiator core assembled in just two minutes. The radiator is mounted on springs to isolate it from flexing in the chassis.

The cooling system of the Model T Ford works on the thermosyphon principle to circulate the water. As the coolant becomes heated it rises in the jacket surrounding the cylinder block and flows into the top of the radiator. From here it falls through the copper tubes where it is cooled by the passing air to be recirculated. A belt-driven fan located behind the radiator ensures a constant flow of air. A drain plug or tap at the bottom of the radiator allows the system to be flushed out.

From the start of production in 1908 until late 1916, the Model T Ford featured a brass radiator. It was replaced with a black-painted pressed steel shell in 1917, known as the 'low' radiator. In late 1923 the radiator was increased in height by 1.4in (3.5cm), from 17.0in (43.2cm) to 18.4in (46.7cm), being known as the 'high' radiator. These were initially black but became nickel-plated on the 'Improved' car from late 1925–27, although nickel plating had already been introduced on UK-produced models in 1924.

Exhaust

The exhaust is attached to one of the chassis side members and connects to the exhaust manifold of the cylinder block.

Fuel tank

The 10 US gallon (38 litre) fuel tank is made from galvanised iron and is located beneath the front seat. No fuel gauge is supplied with the car and so a measuring stick is required

BELOW **Brass radiator.** (*Author*)

BELOW RIGHT **The black pressed-steel radiator can be seen on this 1923 Tourer.** (*Richard Rimmer collection*)

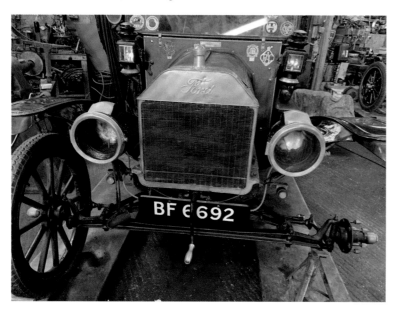

to ascertain how much fuel is in the tank. On
the 'Improved' car in 1925, the fuel tank was
located under the scuttle.

Electrics

Early Model Ts did not have a battery supplied,
but from 1919 a 6V battery, starter and generator
were fitted, with electric horn, headlamps and
tail light. Electric horn and headlamps had
already been introduced from 1914, powered
by the flywheel magneto. Headlamp brightness
depended on the engine speed – if you went too
fast, the bulbs could blow.

Wheels

F ord used wooden, spoked wheels for the
Model T Ford until the introduction of the
'Improved' car in 1927, when wire wheels with
welded spokes were introduced.

The majority of the wheel spokes were made
from shagbark hickory wood, rather than oak
or ash, and up until 1918 the inner part of the
wheel rim, the felloes, was also made from wood.

On early Model Ts, the wheels were not
detachable and the tyres were of the 'beaded-
edge' or 'clincher' type, where the pressure of
the air within the tyre presses it onto the rim
and holds it in place. The disadvantage of this
system is that a tyre cannot be easily changed;
the owner having to jack up the relevant
wheel and use tyre levers to remove the tyre
and repair a puncture at the side of the road,
in the same way as on a bicycle, where the
technology had originated.

'On the beaded-edge tyre, there is a lip,
to which the rim corresponds and grabs it,'
explains Neil Tuckett. 'It hung around well into
the First World War, after which they moved

ABOVE **Wire wheels were introduced on the 1927 'Improved' car.** *(Author)*

BELOW **Beaded-edge rim and tyre.** *(Author)*

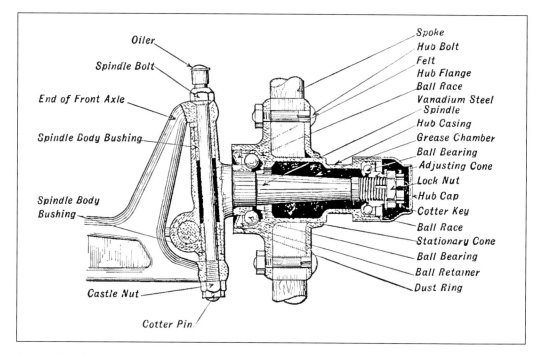

Oiler
Spindle Bolt
End of Front Axle
Spindle Body Bushing
Spindle Body Bushing
Castle Nut
Cotter Pin

Spoke
Hub Bolt
Felt
Hub Flange
Ball Race
Vanadium Steel Spindle
Hub Casing
Grease Chamber
Ball Bearing
Adjusting Cone
Lock Nut
Hub Cap
Cotter Key
Ball Race
Stationary Cone
Ball Bearing
Ball Retainer
Dust Ring

from the beaded-edge rim to a detachable, split rim in 1918.'

Dunlop had developed a straight-edge tyre that slipped onto a spilt-rim wheel and from 1918, Ford supplied wheels with detachable rims. This meant that in the event of a puncture, instead of having to effect a repair at the side of the road, a spare rim and tyre could be carried. Model Ts made in UK, however, were already one step ahead in this regard.

'The English didn't like getting wet and very quickly fitted a detachable wheel with studs in the middle,' explains Neil Tuckett. 'So from

being a fixed wheel vehicle, the English decided to change that, took the whole wheel off and carried a spare. Ford America didn't really cotton on to that for some reason, so by 1918 they put on the detachable rim. Most of the English cars have detachable wheels until the detachable rim came out.'

When the wire wheel came out, it was what is called 'well-based', and the tyre drops into the centre. 'I think Ford was instrumental in developing the wire wheel,' says Neil Tuckett. 'It was originally like a bike wheel, with nipples on the end. He actually spun-welded the spokes in and it all got pre-tensioned with the heat. So the wire wheel, as far as I'm concerned, is quite advanced.

'One of the interesting things relating to Ford,' he continues, 'was that, up until the First World War, most tyres were white. That's how they'd been developed, because rubber is naturally white. But when the war came along they were short of one of the products and they discovered if they put ash or carbon in, it cured the rubber and they became black. That happened in about 1914 and at that point you will see tyres started to become black.'

Painting of the wooden spoked wheels was achieved by dipping each wheel into a vat of paint, raising it until it was just above the paint level, and then spinning it to remove the excess. This was far quicker than painting by hand.

The Ton Trucks were fitted with 30 x 3.5in (76 x 8.9cm)front tyres and 32 x 4.5in 81.3 x 11.4cm) rears, on 23in (58.4cm) rims, although some had solid or 'drilled solid' rear tyres. In 1924–25 this changed to a much wider 6.0in (15.2cm)) and heavier tyre in order to carry the extra weight, while the rear wheel itself got smaller and changed from a 23in to 20in (58.4 to 50.8cm); the fronts remaining the same.

Lighting

Prior to 1915, the headlights of the Model T Ford were powered by acetylene gas. This was supplied from a gas generator carried on the driver's side running board, in which water and calcium carbide combined to produce the gas. A burner in the headlamp itself mixed air with the acetylene.

The generator consists of two compartments: one a water tank and the other containing the calcium carbide. When a shut-off valve, controlled by the driver, is opened, water drips from the upper chamber into the lower chamber through a perforated tube. As the water and calcium carbide combine, acetylene gas is produced along with a residue of lime dust, which collects in the bottom of the generator. The gas is collected in a reservoir and passes through a filter chamber containing wool or similar material to the headlamp.

After 1915, the cars were fitted with electric headlamps, powered by the Ford magneto, which had been redesigned to carry larger magnets and produce a greater current. From 1919, a 6V electrical system was provided, which was used to power the headlamps plus a single tail lamp. From 1925 an optional brake lamp was available.

The original Model T Fords also came supplied with three oil lamps: two at the bottom of the windscreen and one at the rear.

'Initially, Ford didn't give you lights, and windscreens were optional,' explains Neil Tuckett, 'but quite quickly he started upgrading and both windscreens and lights came along. Headlights were acetylene, and the side and rear lights were oil. The gas was produced like in a miner's lamp, with calcium carbide in a container, dripping water, and you had to control it, which is why the acetylene generator is down beside

LEFT The acetylene generator is located on the running board. The driver uses a shut-off valve which controls the amount of water dripping onto the calcium carbide. *(Author)*

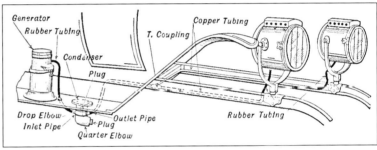

ABOVE **Acetylene gas lighting system.** *(Pagé)*

BELOW **Electric headlamps were fitted after 1915.** *(Author)*

the driver, so he could lean over and vary it. So that would be the left or right side depending on left- or right-hand drive. It can be a bit of a faff, and had a habit of going bang. It was a primitive system but used known technology.

'By 1911, the accessory manufacturers had developed an acetylene bottle which was pumped up and you didn't have to muck around with calcium carbide,' he continues. 'By 1915, Ford had gone on to electric headlights

running off the magneto and retained the oil lights on the rear and the side.

'That wasn't very successful, insomuch as the magneto was very limited on power and if it wasn't in good condition you didn't get lights. But the biggest problem was that the magneto produced between eight and thirty volts, depending on the speed of the engine. When you came to a road junction, you slowed down, so your engine slowed, the lights would dim and you couldn't see anything. So you had to leave it revving its backside off to read the signs.

'Up to that point Ford hadn't provided a battery but he left a position for one, so you could go and buy a battery after you had bought a car. By 1918, when the starter motor and the dynamo came out, a battery was supplied. They were pretty primitive to be fair, but they worked. It would have been an expensive item, though, and Ford actually produced a booklet telling the customers how they could build their own battery.'

Tools, spare parts and accessories

Tools

The Ford owner was expected to carry out his own maintenance and so each car came equipped with a rudimentary toolkit. This consisted of:

- A tyre pump
- Pliers
- Screwdriver
- Spark plug/cylinder head/wheel spanner
- Adjustable spanner
- Tyre tools and patch kit
- Band adjusting spanner
- Combination hub cap, front wheel bearing and nut axle spanner

Note: Spark plugs were very expensive and so, rather than replacing them, a spark plug would be taken apart, carefully cleaned and then reassembled before the gap was set. For this reason, the Model T Ford spark plug spanner was double-ended. One end was used to remove the plug from the cylinder, while the other was for removing the nut that held the porcelain inside the plug.

Spare parts

Spare parts for the Model T Ford were made readily available at the time of its manufacture and can still be easily obtained through specialist outlets today.

'Sometime around 1928–30,' explains Chris Barker, 'Henry Ford said something along the lines of, "We will not let Model T owners down. Even if Model Ts last ten years, we will supply them with spares." That is indicative of how long people expected cars to last then.'

Replacement or alternative parts were also widely available from third-party manufacturers. 'I'm of the belief that you could buy every single part of a Model T from other people,' claims Neil Tuckett. 'I have never seen an advert for a chassis though, that's the only thing I've never seen, but everything else was available.'

Accessories

One immediate offshoot from the Model T Ford was the development of an extensive aftermarket supply of accessories of every kind. Manufacturers offered items such as bumpers, which Ford didn't offer until 1926, heaters, hoods, exhaust horns, carburettors and all sorts of parts designed to 'transform your Ford'.

In their book, *Farewell To Model T*, Richard Lee Strout and E.B. White wrote:

> *The purchaser never regarded his purchase as a complete, finished product. When you bought a Ford, you figured you had a start – a vibrant, spirited framework to which could be screwed an almost limitless assortment of decorative and functional hardware.*

'You could say that the Model T gave rise to the entire aftermarket business, or accessory market,' explains Chris Barker, 'especially as Ford thought what left the factory was perfect and needed no embellishments or modifications or additions. So you had these huge catalogues published in the '20s for everything that you could imagine – bodies, engine parts, suspension modifications and so on.

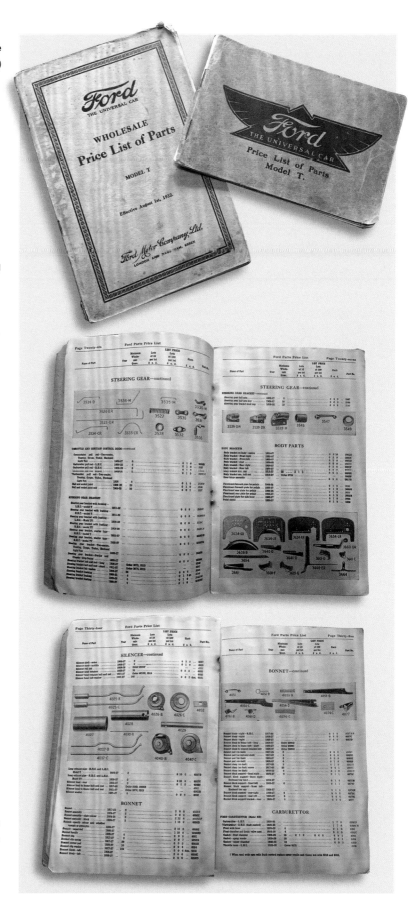

DOUBLE the { STRENGTH USEFULNESS CAPACITY } OF YOUR FORD

with the

BAICO

MAKE-A-TRUCK

£75

Complete with solid rear Tyres, Brakes, Sprockets, and Chains.

ONE TON CAPACITY
(British Made).

No Expert Fitting Required.

Wheelbase, 11 feet.
Takes 13ft. 6in. Body.

Send for Illustrations of British Installations and Types of Bodies.

BRITISH-AMERICAN IMPORT COMPANY, Ltd.,
11a, HAYMARKET, LONDON, S.W. 1.

'In the '20s there were three or four well-known suppliers of modified engine components, overhead valve conversions, even overhead cam conversions, 16-valve heads. There are quite a lot of those left today and they're quite sought after and expensive. They put the power of the engine up from 20hp to 50hp or 60hp.

'If you thumb through the catalogues, you'll see mirrors, snow chains, aftermarket non-factory spares, horns, tyre pumps, different lamps, different hoods, even different crankshafts, modifications to the ignition system and timers. There were as many timer designs as there were cars. Henry Ford's view on all this was "Don't do it".

'There was even an accessory that converted your car into a truck, by way of extending the wheelbase with a chassis extension. A chain drive geared down from the car's axle and it proved very popular. It was what spurred Ford into making the Ton Truck.' (See Chapter Seven – Endless Varieties.)

Ford may have tried to discourage owners from purchasing aftermarket accessories, but he sometimes forced them into doing just that, as Neil Tuckett explains.

'Up until 1918 there was no starter motor,

you just swung the handle,' he said. 'From 1918 onwards it was an option, then it became standard, except on the Ton Truck. In the UK you couldn't buy a Ton Truck with a starter motor, because it took it over the weight limit for horsepower taxation. You had to buy the starter motor after you'd bought the truck, whereas in the car, it became standard.

'That was good old Ford, he played the system. But with horsepower tax in the UK it took the Model T off the road because it was 22.5 RAC hp, whereas the Austin Seven was six or seven, and it was £1 per horsepower, so the tax, rounded up, was £23 per year, equivalent to £1,200 today. So car sales dropped but the truck sales rose, because he was the only manufacturer who produced a truck weighing under one tonne that could carry one tonne, whereas the Morris was 13cwt (660kg) to carry a tonne, so they were paying bigger tax rates.

'Most accessories were a good idea that made no difference,' he added. 'And some of them are the most stupid accessories. I saw one called a batometer. What the hell's a batometer? It was a gauge to tell you how much water was in your battery and what the condition of the battery was. There was no way it worked. Gradient meters as well. You name it!'

ELLISON & CO.

Commutators, Magnetos, Conversion Set, etc.—Ford Section

TURNER 2-in-1 TIMER

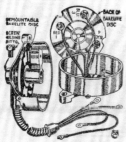

Accurate and simple. Give instant "start-up" in zero weather. Saves 10% to 15% petrol consumption. No oiling. All parts interchangeable
List No. YE/4450 Complete .. **22/6**

TURNER TIMER SPARE PARTS
List No. YE/4451

Rotor Assembly complete .. each **5/3**
Contact Brush, Special Bronze each **2/-**
Contact Brush Spring .. .. each **9d.**
Timer Disc and Shell complete each **13/-**
Timer Wire Assembly complete each **10/3**

TUNGSTEN CONTACT POINTS AND SPRINGS

List No. YG/4462
per pair **1/-**

IMPROVED ELECTRON BRUSH

Instead of roller on Ford commutator.

Never wears out the commutator.
List No. YE/4464 .. each **2/6**

GENUINE KW COIL UNIT

With Tungsten Points
List No. YG/4463
each **11/-**

"CHAMPION DE LUXE" TIMER

Everlasting wear. Wipe contact by means of solid copper brush on flat track. Unbreakable. "Short proof." Functions without oil. All parts cheaply renewable. R. or L. hand drive.
List No. YK/4466 .. .. each **8/6**

"CHAMPION" REPLACEMENT PARTS
List No. YK/4467

Complete Brush Assembly (De Luxe) each **3/6**
Ditto (Popular) .. .. each **3/6**
Brushes and Springs, complete doz. **7/9**

SILENT CHAIN-DRIVE CONVERSION

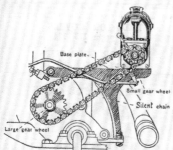

"BOSCH" SPIRAL GEAR DRIVE
Complete with FU4 Magneto, with Control, plug wires, and Switch.
List No. YEN/4459 .. the set **£14 12 6**

SET FOR CAMSHAFT
For Ford Cars

Fittings complete for Camshaft Drive using Silent Chain. The Set comprises cast aluminium bracket, magneto sprocket bored to fit spindle, Camshaft sprocket bored.
List No. YG/4452
With Silent Chain and
Control **40/-**

Sundry Parts
List No. YG/4453 Platform **12/-**
List No. YG/4454 Chains **15/-**
List No. YG/4455
Large Sprockets **9/-**
List No. YG/4456
Small Sprockets **6/-**
List No. YG/4457
Sets Bolts and Nuts, per set **2/8**
List No. YG/4458 Controls **3/6**

MAGNETOS

For particulars and prices of Magnetos for use with the Magneto Conversion Sets shown on this page, see pages 139 and 140

When ordering "Conversion" Sets it is very important to state if right or left hand drive model is required.

BOWDEN MAGNETO CONTROL
No. 492
(Ford Pattern)

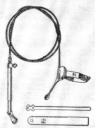

Specially designed to suit the Ford Car, on which a Magneto replaces the usual type of Ford ignition.
List No. YG/4468 .. each **15/6**

"W. & D." MAGNETO CONVERSION SETS

To suit either starter or non-starter type Fords. Fitted with Vernier Adjustable Coupling. Made for Clockwise or Anti-Clockwise Magnetos. Without Magneto.

List No. YG/4460 Complete .. **70/-**

BOSCH FF4 MAGNETO

Centre, 38 m/m., complete with baseplate, suitable for Conversion Sets.
List No. YEN/4461 .. .. **£8 2 0**

MAGNETO SET FOR FORDSONS

List No. YG/4465
Camshaft Drive.. .. .. per set **35/-**
Do., with Coventry Silent Chain per set **60/-**
Oil Filler Pipe extra if required each **22/-**

"STADIUM" SPARKTESTER
Neon Gasfilled

Any ignition trouble the Neon Gas-filled "Sparktester" will diagnose accurately and quickly. Fitted with vest pocket clip it can be carried in the same manner as a fountain pen and always handy for use.
Overall length 3 ins., diameter ⅝ ins. A thoroughly reliable tester at a popular price.

List No. YK/4469

Model 745. Complete with instructions for use .. .. each **1/6**

One dozen Testers supplied on attractive two-colour display card, as illustrated .. .. per card **18/-**

123/5 ALBION St., LEEDS & 15 CUMBERLAND St., DEANSGATE, MANCHESTER

ELLISON & CO.

Oil Gauges, Radiators, Shock Absorbers, Screens, etc.—Ford Section

"T. & M." OIL GAUGE
For Model "A" Fords

Indicates oil flow and low level in crank-case. Is of N.P. finish with black dial, and is very easily installed. A necessity on both the cars and trucks.
List No. YG/4500 .. .. .. each **19/6**

"NEVAJAHS"

Set X. For cars with 2 spring clips. (For cars with single spring clip order Set Y).
Inexpensive, efficient, simple. Makes riding luxurious. No drilling or adapting.

List No.			Each
YG/4501 Car (front)	..	..	**15/6**
YG/4502 Car (rear)	..	..	**90/-**
YG/4503 Van (front)	..	..	**16/9**
YG/4504 Van (rear)	..	..	**105/-**

"GRAFTON" SIDE CURTAINS FOR FORD VANS

Fit 7 cwt. or 1 ton Standard Ford Vans, 1916 to latest.

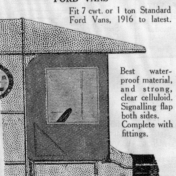

Best waterproof material, and strong, clear celluloid. Signalling flap both sides. Complete with fittings.

Type 205 (as illustrated). Flexible type, with holding clip when rolled up.
List No. YG/4505 .. .. .. per pair **25/-**
Type 303. Rigid Type, open and close with doors. Instantly detachable.
List No. YG/4506 .. .. .. per pair **9/6**

"EASYFILL" LOCKING RADIATOR CAP
For Model "A" Ford Cars

Screws on to Radiator just like the ordinary cap, and locked by means of the set screw, becoming a permanent fixture. Hinged cap for refilling. Cap is N.P. non-rusting finish, and is supplied ready to take temperature meter or ornament. An ornamental steel bolt (as illustrated) can be supplied.
List No. YG/4507 N.P. Cap .. .. each **15/-**
List No. YG/4508 Ornamental Bolt .. each **1/6**

FORD MOTO-METER

For Cars prior to 1928.
All N.P. with Ford Radiator Cap.
List No. YG/4509 .. .. .. each **16/6**

SUPER RIGID SIDE SCREENS

For Ford Van, One-Ton Truck, and One-Ton Van. Easily fitted by means of screws only. Open and shut with door. Perfectly rigid and draughtproof.
List No. YG/4510 Complete **37/6**

"MIDLAND" RADIATOR

Type "R"
Interchangeable with 1917/26 Type Fords. Detachable Cast Aluminium Units.—Guaranteed Non-corrosive Metal.
Block.—S.D. Gilled Copper (not brass), each row strongly stayed.
Road Tests.—Load 25 cwts. 60 miles. No stop. No boil. Guaranteed five years
List No. YG/4511
Type P (with plain top) **£7 10 0**
Type R 1924/1926 .. .. **£8 0 0**
All polished finished, 5/- extra.

IMPORTANT

When ordering Radiators, state clearly year of Car or Van, and finish required.

RADIATOR COVERS
See pages 173, 174

RADIATOR HOSE CLIPS,
See pages 85, 86

FORD RADIATOR CAPS

Model 902. Standard Pattern (as illustrated).
List No. YG/4512 N.P. .. .. per doz. **9/2**
List No. YG/4513 Polished Brass per doz. **8/8**
Model 903. Hexagon Ebonite Top.
List No. YG/4514 .. .. .. each **1/9**
Model 904. Round Fluted Top.
List No. YG/4515 .. .. .. each **2/-**

RADIATOR HOSE

Ford Type, Moulded Ends.		List No. YG/4516	
Inlet, 2¾" long × 1⅜"	**1/-**	.. per doz.	**9/-**
Outlet, 3½" long × 2"	**1/-**	.. per doz.	**11/-**
Outlet, 4" long × 2"	**1/-**	.. per doz.	**12/-**

123/5 ALBION St., LEEDS & 15 CUMBERLAND St., DEANSGATE, MANCHESTER

ELLISON & CO.

Speedometers, Springs, Shims, Gaskets, Tipping Gear, etc.—Ford Section

"STEWART" SPEEDOMETER

Specially designed for Model T Ford.
List No. YG/4550 .. .. £3 15 0

"LAMINUM" BRASS SHIM

As one solid piece, but can be peeled with a knife, being laminated .002".

List No. YG/4551	Thickness	$\frac{1}{64}$	$\frac{1}{32}$	$\frac{1}{16}$
				per dozen
Connecting Rod, Fordson Tractor		3/3	5/6	11/6
Main Bearing. Fordson Tractor ..		6/-	10/-	19/-

List No. YG/4552	Thickness	$\frac{1}{64}$	$\frac{1}{32}$
Connecting Rod Ford Car	..	2/8	5/6
Front and Centre Crankshaft, Ford Car	3/3	6/6
Crankshaft, Rear, Ford Car	..	5/6	10/-

List No. YG/4553 **Complete Sets 14 Shims**
$\frac{1}{64}$" thick .. .. set 4/6
$\frac{1}{32}$ " .. .. set 7/6

STOCK SHEETS, 6″ × 36″

	List No. YG/4554		Per lb.
A	$\frac{1}{64}$", $\frac{1}{32}$", $\frac{1}{16}$" All Laminated '002"	..	15/6
B	$\frac{1}{16}$", $\frac{1}{2}$ Laminated and $\frac{1}{2}$ Solid '002"		14/9
C	$\frac{1}{16}$"	,, ,, ,, '002"	12/6
D	$\frac{1}{32}$"	,, ,, ,, '002"	12/9
E	$\frac{1}{32}$"	,, ,, ,, '002"	13/3
F	$\frac{1}{32}$"	,, ,, ,, '002"	12/6

CYLINDER HEAD GASKETS

In Copper and Asbestos

List No.			Each
YG/4555	Best quality ..	..	2/4
YG/4556	Standard quality..	..	1/6
YK/4557	Do. in $\frac{1}{2}$-gross lots	..	1/6
YG/4558	Fordson ..	..	8/-

"BOB" FORD GASKET

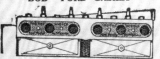

The now improved Six-Way "C. & A." Gasket replaces the usual six loose ring washers, it saves time and endless trouble in fixing. Once fitted it cannot fall or become displaced.
List No. JK/4559 .. .. .. per doz. 18/-

VAN OR TONNER HUBOMETER

Brass hub cap with Recorder. Either front wheel.
List No. YG/4560 .. .. each £1 17 6
N.P. Finish 2/6 extra.

Worm Drive Type

Fits in place of existing cover at back of worm.
List No. YG/4561 .. .. each 60/-
State if for high or low speed.

BRASS SHIMS FOR THE FORD

Model 291MA. Packets of 300 Bearing Shims, containing 200 Shims for connecting rod bearings, 50 Shims for crankshaft front and centre bearings, 50 Shims for crankshaft rear bearings. All made from Annealed Brass Shim Stock .003" thick.

List No. YG/4562 .. .. per packet 6/3
List No. YG/4563 Separate Shims. Per 100

Model 391	Connecting Rod Shims	..	2/-
Model 392	Crankshaft front and centre bearing shims	..	2/4
Model 393	Crankshaft rear bearing shims		2/8

CORK GASKETS

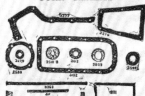

	List No. YG/4564	Per 100
A	Axle Outer Roller Big Washer	7/6
B	Ball Cup Gasket	15/-
C	Cyl. Cover	11/-
D	Crankcase and Cyl. Gasket, left	16/-
E	" " right	16/-
F	" Lower Cover Gasket	50/-
G	Cyl. Valve Cover Gasket	12/-
H	"	38/4
I	Commutator Ring Gasket	6/6
J	Trans. Cover Gasket, front	10/-
K	"	37/6
L	" Sloping Door Gasket	23/6
M	Bendix Cover Gasket ..	7/-

SHEET CORK

List No. YG/4565 36″ × 12″ × $\frac{1}{16}$" ea. 2/-

SPRINGS FOR FORDS

List No. YG/4566, 9 leaf, rear .. .. each 28/-
List No. YG/4567, 8 leaf, front .. .. each 10/6
List No. YG/4568, **Tonner** Springs .. each 16/9
Doz. lots of above subject to discount K.

SPRING PERCH   High Patt.

Better distribution of weights when heavy loads are carried.
List No. YG/4569, Tonners and Van, rear .. per pair 9/-
List No. YG/4570, Ton Truck, rear .. .. per pair 7/6
List No. YG/4571, All Models, front .. .. per pair 9/-

CRANK-CASE REPAIR ARM

STENTOPHONE CRANK-CASE REPAIR ARM.

Replaces broken arm without dismantling crank-case, and makes a reliable job.
List No. YG/4572 .. .. .. each 2/6

"AUSTER" SPRING PUTTEES
For Fords

List No. YG/4573 .. .. per outfit 20/-

"QUIKKO" TIPPING GEAR (Jennings' Patent)

Tipper is improved since illustrated.

With this Tipping Gear a standard Ford Vehicle can be converted into an easily manipulated tipping wagon. Can be fitted in a few moments without any alteration to the body or chassis. Compact, remarkably strong, and will last a lifetime. Gear can be operated from either side.

The Tipping Gear showing Levers in action. They will raise 1 ton in 20 seconds.
List No. YG/4574, Complete £6 0 0
Type for New 30 cwt. Model Ford, similar to above. Light, strong, and takes up no body space.
List No. YG/4574a.. .. .. complete £7 15 0
For other patterns Tipping Gear see page **40** General List.

123/5 ALBION St., LEEDS & 15 CUMBERLAND St., DEANSGATE, MANCHESTER

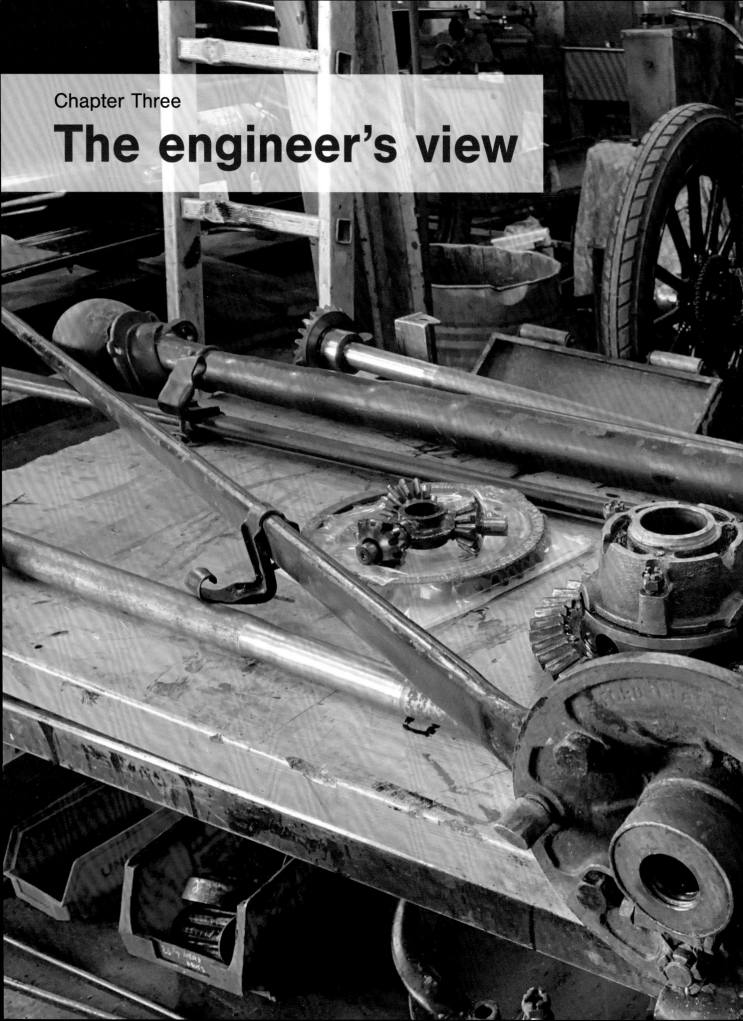

Chapter Three
The engineer's view

Chris Barker – The engineering legacy of the Model T Ford

In 2015, Chris Barker, archivist of the Model T Ford Register of Great Britain, gave a lecture to the Newcomen Society at the Science Museum, London, about the engineering legacy of the Model T Ford. The following is based in part upon the contents of that lecture:

■ The basic layout of the Model T Ford – engine at the front, rear-wheel drive, a simple rectangular chassis with a wheel at each corner, all mechanical parts within the

RIGHT A plan view showing the general layout and main components of the car. *(Pagé)*

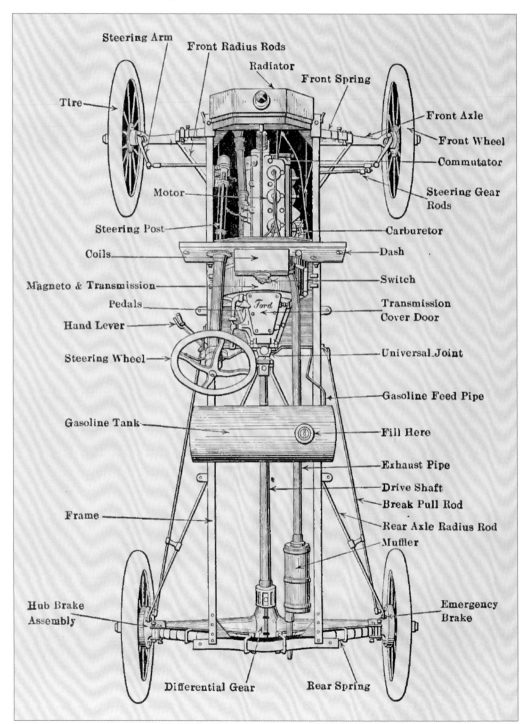

OPPOSITE TOP A right-hand side view showing the main details...

OPPOSITE BOTTOM ... and similarly, a left-hand side view. *(both Pagé)*

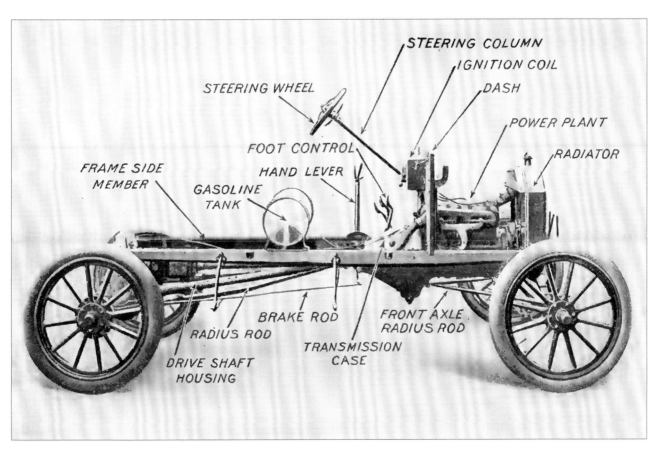

STEERING COLUMN

IGNITION COIL

STEERING WHEEL

DASH

POWER PLANT

RADIATOR

FOOT CONTROL

FRAME SIDE MEMBER

HAND LEVER

GASOLINE TANK

BRAKE ROD

FRONT AXLE RADIUS ROD

RADIUS ROD

TRANSMISSION CASE

DRIVE SHAFT HOUSING

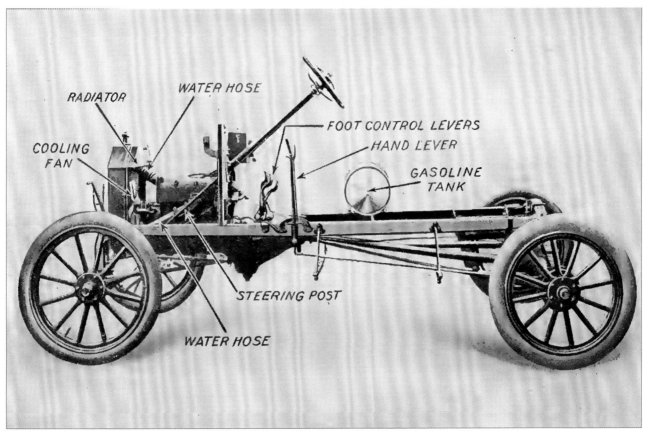

RADIATOR

WATER HOSE

COOLING FAN

FOOT CONTROL LEVERS

HAND LEVER

GASOLINE TANK

STEERING POST

WATER HOSE

wheelbase of the car, radiator over the front axle, fuel central, four seats – is certainly a layout that became the norm.

■ The suspension and steering, however, while being innovative, did not catch on (although its features persisted in later small Fords until the 1950s). The suspension comprised a single transverse leaf spring at each end, and no damping apart from that caused by the friction between the leaves of the spring. A solid axle at each end, well located by radius rods running back to the engine, provided a lot of travel and therefore a reasonable ride over the early roads of the time. It should be remembered, also, that in many places the Model T preceded roads and caused them to be built. Ford claimed that the three-point attachment system stopped the chassis from twisting, but this was not the case. It may have been softer in roll, tolerable with the wide track.

■ The steering was simple but ingenious, using an epicyclic gearbox in the hub of the steering wheel to provide a reduction of either 4:1 or 5:1. It was not a system that was developed

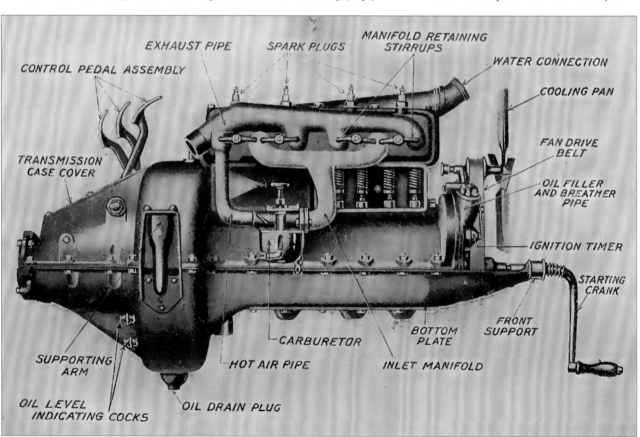

or used subsequently, though, and it allowed anti-self-centring when reversing.

- The wheels themselves were conventional for the time and not detachable for the first ten years of the Model T's life. Later cars had detachable rims, but detachable wheels became the norm.

- The four-cylinder single block, detachable head, three-bearing engine design (excluding the trembler coil ignition) became the pattern of almost all 'ordinary' car engines, such as those from Ford, Morris, Austin and Hillman, up until the 1950s. Many early engines featured separate or paired cylinder castings and fixed cylinder heads. In 1908 there was a variety of surface carbs and other devices Ford could have used, but he selected a simple and reliable conventional carburettor.

- Henry Ford did not want a battery on the Model T. High-tension magnetos were available, but they were expensive and not reliable. Magnetos would also have meant him paying royalties for their use – something he didn't want to do. Trembler coils were fairly common, but use of them was decreasing. Ford's solution (also seen on the earlier Model N) was to use an alternator (which he confusingly called a magneto) mounted on the flywheel. It comprised 16 magnets mounted on the flywheel and 16 coils wound onto a pressed steel plate on the back of the engine. So there were 16 cycles for every revolution of the engine. This provided around five volts at idle, rising to over thirty volts at speed. The location of the magnets controlled the timing, so the spark lever only chose which peak. Starting is much easier with a battery to power the coils temporarily.

- In 1919, Ford added an electric starter, apparently for the benefit of the increasing number of female drivers, and therefore also a generator and battery. The six-volt system was very conventional but for reasons known only to himself, Ford elected to retain the magneto and trembler coils, when he could have opted for a distributor and coil, saving a considerable amount of money and improving the reliability.

- Fuel was gravity-fed from a tank under the front seat and it was important to keep the tank full, otherwise the cars would come to

a stop when going uphill due to fuel-feed problems. The location of the fuel tank meant that passengers had to get out when the car was being refuelled. From 1926, the last Model Ts to be built featured a scuttle tank, higher up, and an external filler.

- A handbrake operated, via rods, on rear brake drums, but these were not lined and not very effective until the later cars.

- As far as the transmission goes, the rear axle and the differential were conventional, but included a torque tube – a rigid casing with a slender drive shaft, all enclosed. The gears were epicyclic, with no sliding pinions or dogs, with just two forward gears. Top was direct and engaged by a multiplate clutch, while low and reverse gears were controlled by contracting bands moved directly by pedals on the casing. Three triple planetary gears were located on pegs on the flywheel, their motion controlled by stopping one of the sun gears connected to the drums and bands. The low sun gear is smaller than the output gear, hence a low forward gear. The reverse sun gear is larger than the output gear, so a low reverse gear.

- The early gearboxes, with sliding pinions, were very difficult to use and as long as you have never driven any other car, the Model T is very, very easy to drive – you can't crunch gears.

- It should be stressed that epicyclic gears were not new and had been used on many early American cars, including the Curved-Dash Oldsmobile, probably the first mass-produced car. All of Fred Lanchester's pre-First World War cars also had epicyclic gears, and Ford is known to have bought a 1905 Lanchester. This form of transmission reappeared in the Wilson and Cotal gearboxes of the 1930s, in the post-war Laycock OD and in most automatic gearboxes until recent times.
- The service brake, located on a third drum on the output shaft, was just about adequate and it was just possible to lock the rear wheels should the need arise. There were never any front brakes on the Model T.
- The engine and transmission were carried in a large steel pressing. Its three-point mounting prevented chassis deflections transferring forces to the engine. The gearbox was covered by a casting, so the whole unit was sealed (give or take the odd drip). This is standard now, but in 1908 it wasn't usual practice. Cars would have a total loss system, the gearbox displaced two feet back from the engine with a shaft joining them and an exposed clutch, open to the road grit and goodness knows what else.

- It was unusual to offer a range of standard bodies, since most cars had coach-built bodies, except for Lanchester. This, of course, later became the norm.
- Good quality steel, including vanadium alloys, were used where appropriate. What is less well-known is that, although vanadium steel was used extensively during the early life of the Model T, by the 1920s they had moved onto other alloys and treatments because cars had been suffering fatigue failures in crankshafts and half-shafts. This was all part of an ongoing product development.
- There was some use of aluminium in the early cars, such as the gearbox cover casting, bonnet and body panels. Fasteners were standardised and mostly what later became unified fine thread (UNF), with some coarse (UNC). There was a full interchangeability of parts between cars and later parts were often interchangeable with earlier types.
- The design was intended for large-scale efficient manufacture and was evolved as time passed.

To summarise, so many aspects of the Model T later became the industry norm, if only for a while. These were: basic dimensions; range of factory bodies; side-valve four-cylinder, single-casting block engine with detachable head; sealed unit-construction engine/gearbox; excellent materials (saving weight); innovative manufacturing processes (especially pressings); and continuous product development.

What did not survive was: the two-speed gearbox; trembler coils and magneto; transmission brake; gravity-fed fuel from under the seat; only black cars.

Neil Tuckett

With over 30 years' experience, Neil Tuckett is an acknowledged world expert on pre-1930s Fords.

'Because the car was built over such a long length of time, if it wasn't right it became right, and it can't have been wrong because they built 15 million. But there were technical improvements going on every single day. It is a big Meccano kit, and it certainly was robust through the quality of materials and the simplicity. It became quite

CONTROL PEDAL ASSEMBLY

TOP HALF OF GEAR CASE

MAGNETO TERMINAL

SLOW SPEED BAND ADJUSTMENT

RIGHT Removing the transmission cover for access to the brake bands. *(Pagé)*

obvious that you could repair them on the side of the road or in the field, which is what happened. They set up a dealer network throughout the world very quickly. I think in America by 1910 or 1911 they had 19,000 dealers. The car had only been on the road for three years at that point, and the same in the UK. The dealer network became a big money-spinner.

The first big change that he came up with was that he cast the engine block in one piece. Prior to 1908 all the car manufacturers basically built a sump and bolted on cylinders. Ford had a cast block and cast head, which he put together. So that was the biggest thing. He came up with what we call a magneto, it's not what the vintage car boys know as a magneto but it's a power source inside the engine. So on the flywheel, there's a set of 16 magnets which go past coils, and that produces power. He didn't give a battery initially. You had to spin the engine to get power, and that produced power to produce a spark.

A lot of his innovations had actually come back a hundred years later. For example, each spark plug has a coil rather than one coil doing the whole job. Today, most cars have a coil per spark plug.

The lightweight construction was very advanced for its time, as was the simplicity – no water pump, no oil pump. Hot water rises and oil splashes, it's that simple.

With a Model T Ford, I think the saying, "if it ain't broke, don't fix it" really applies. Leave it alone and run it. The more you run it, the more you iron out any little niggle, whether it's dirt in the fuel or whatever, and it's done for another ten years, or another generation. The ones that don't run well are the ones that sit in a garage or museums. Museum buys are the worst. They're really shiny and they're either worn out or mechanically in trouble.

The whole of the Model T is based on three-point suspensions. You've got the engine – three points, front axle – three points, back axle – three points, and it all pivots round a flexing chassis and a big universal joint in the middle. It worked. It was designed to move. The first of the bodies were built with wood, aluminium and steel, and eventually the bodies became spot-welded together. So the bodies became more and more rigid as time went on, but Ford intended everything to move for the rough conditions.

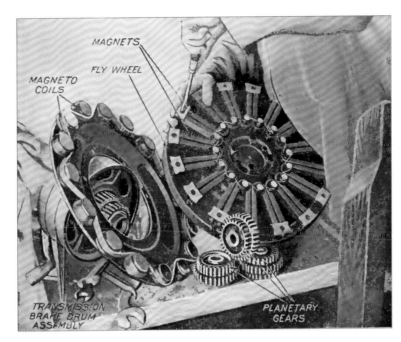

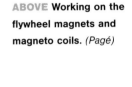

In 1924, the UK-manufactured Model Ts were lowered, two years ahead of America, because our roads were much better. I think Ford allowed them to experiment because it didn't make financial sense to produce the few cars over here that had been lowered for the cost of doing it, but Ford obviously thought, "that worked", and took the idea back to America. So the drop-frame cars in England were two or three years ahead of the American cars.'

ABOVE Working on the flywheel magnets and magneto coils. *(Pagé)*

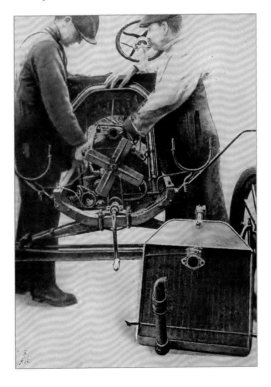

LEFT With the radiator removed, engine removal is a lot easier than on many later vehicles! *(Pagé)*

Chapter Four

The driver's view

'The Model T is easy to drive... as long as you have never driven anything else!'

Chris Barker
Archivist, Model T Ford Register of Great Britain

View from the passenger seat and the open road ahead. *(Author)*

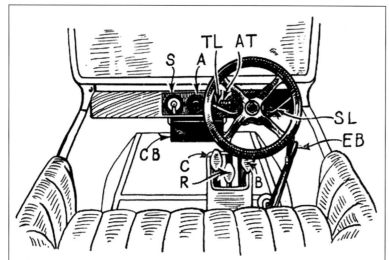

View of driving compartment showing controls, etc. A, ammeter. B, brake pedal. C, clutch pedal. R, reverse pedal. S, switch. AT, air-throttle. CB, coil-box. EB, emergency brake lever. SL, spark lever. TL, throttle lever.

ABOVE The controls of a right-hand-drive Model T Ford. *(Chris Barker collection)*

The controls

Mounted on the steering wheel of the Model T Ford are the spark and throttle levers. On a left-hand-drive model, the spark lever is on the left and the throttle is on the right. These positions are reversed on a right-hand-drive car. The throttle lever controls the amount of fuel drawn into the engine, while the spark lever controls the timing of the spark to ensure that the fuel and air mixture ignites at the correct moment. Each lever moves through a 90° arc in a series of notches.

On the floor are three pedals. The left-hand pedal controls the high- and low-speed gears. The middle pedal is for reverse and the right-hand pedal is the footbrake.

The hand lever to the side of the driver engages the high-speed clutch when it is in its forward-most position. In its centre position, it engages neutral but does not apply the rear hub brakes. Fully back, it is in neutral with the brakes applied.

Starting the Model T Ford

To start a Model T, the first task is to turn on the fuel tap, which is located under the fuel tank, and ensure the ignition is turned off. The spark lever should be fully retarded (pushed up) and the throttle set about three or four notches down. If the spark is advanced too far, the engine might kick back when being cranked over, resulting in injury (to driver or starter motor!). The handbrake lever should be pulled back as far as possible, which releases

RIGHT On early cars, up to about 1915, the three floor-mounted pedals are conveniently labelled C, R and B, for clutch, reverse and brake. *(Author)*

the clutch and applies the hub brakes, and the switch on the coil box set to 'magneto' for cars with no battery, or 'battery' when one is fitted. The car is now fully prepared to be started.

Grasping the starting handle in one hand, with the thumb on the same side of the handle as the fingers, it should be cranked upwards in one quick movement, at which point, with luck, the engine will burst into life. Once it is running, the spark lever should be advanced to its halfway position and the engine allowed to run until it is warmed up.

To set off, the left-hand pedal should be held in its centre position and the handbrake released by moving the lever all the way forward. The throttle should be pulled back a little and the left-hand pedal pushed slowly all the way to the floor to select the low speed. When the car has achieved a speed of around 12mph (19kph), the throttle should be closed, the left pedal brought up into the high-speed position and the throttle opened again quite quickly. To stop, the throttle should be closed, the left pedal pushed to its halfway position, and the right-hand pedal (brake) pushed fully down.

To select low speed while driving, slow down to less than 15mph (24kph) by closing the

throttle. Slowly press the left pedal fully down and hold it down, controlling the speed with the throttle.

To reverse, the car should be brought to a stop and the clutch disengaged by moving the handbrake lever to its midway position. The centre pedal is then pushed down slowly to reverse the car.

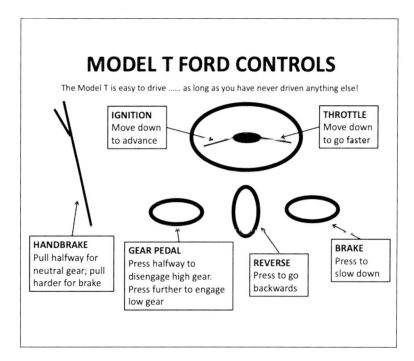

MODEL T FORD CONTROLS

The Model T is easy to drive ...... as long as you have never driven anything else!

IGNITION
Move down to advance

THROTTLE
Move down to go faster

HANDBRAKE
Pull halfway for neutral gear; pull harder for brake

GEAR PEDAL
Press halfway to disengage high gear. Press further to engage low gear

REVERSE
Press to go backwards

BRAKE
Press to slow down

ABOVE Instructions for driving a Model T Ford.
(Chris Barker collection)

LEFT Once underway, speed is controlled by the throttle lever mounted under the steering wheel. *(Author)*

The driving experience

So what's a Model T Ford like to drive? 'Different, but very simple,' is Neil Tuckett's answer. 'It's basically an automatic gearbox that is controlled with pedals and clutches. A primitive automatic gearbox.'

And what about comfort? 'Air conditioning is free,' he laughs. 'And heating is by removing the floorboards to expose the exhaust pipe! Heaters were available as an accessory in the enclosed cars in the form of a grille to allow heat in. They're as comfortable as you want to make them. They're not uncomfortable, unless you're very tall, in which case the later the model, the harder it is to get in and out. The Centredoor is good for a tall person because the roof is quite high.'

The Model T is also quite comfortable and easy to drive, sitting in traffic. 'It's no different to an automatic,' says Neil. 'Press the pedal when you want to go forward or take your foot off to find neutral and it won't go anywhere, it's that simple. It's not prone to overheating, though that's down to maintenance. Yes, it could overheat if the radiator is blocked or dying of old age, but it's completely practical and useable.'

As explained in Chapter Two (see page 59), when starting a Model T in the cold, it is advisable to jack up one of the rear wheels to prevent it from creeping forward when the handle is turned over.

DRIVING LESSON

Neil Tuckett runs driving courses every year and reckons that, quite quickly, nine out of ten drivers can be taught to drive a Model T. 'We have a good turnout and pretty well, without exception, we teach them to drive,' he said. 'But it is different, because you have three pedals that are not doing what you are expecting them to do. Once you've had a panic it's usually all right though...'

So how long does it take to teach someone? 'Children: ten minutes, because they listen,' he answered. 'Adults: probably an hour. And then, after about a hundred miles you will naturally jump in it and just do it normally.'

We didn't have an hour to spare on my visit, so I was given a very brief lesson down Neil's farm track. The first surprise on driving a Model T Ford for the first time was how smooth everything was. The one thing I kept telling myself was to concentrate on the steering wheel-mounted throttle and to remember that was how to control the speed. The second was that the right-hand pedal was the brake. Keeping those two things in mind, and repeating them to myself, made it seem a lot less daunting as I set off down the track.

As we gathered speed, I took my foot off the left-hand pedal in order to engage high gear and felt momentarily apprehensive as the car sped up, but by easing the throttle lever back a little, I quickly felt that I was going at a speed that was comfortable for me. The steering was responsive and everything, as I said, felt very smooth.

The odd thing is that, once you are on your way, there is little to do. Control the speed with the throttle, use the brake as necessary and steer in the right line – it's very much like driving a car with an automatic gearbox, the only difference being that, with a conventional car, you take your foot off the accelerator in order to press the brake pedal. With the Model T Ford it is worth remembering to push the throttle lever back a little as you brake, and then accelerate again when required.

My experience benefitted from the fact that there was no other traffic to contend with and that I had the farm track to myself. Driving a Model T on the open road must be a very different experience, having to concentrate both on other road users and the unfamiliar controls at the same time. But I loved it!

LEFT The author gets behind the wheel.
(Neil Tuckett)

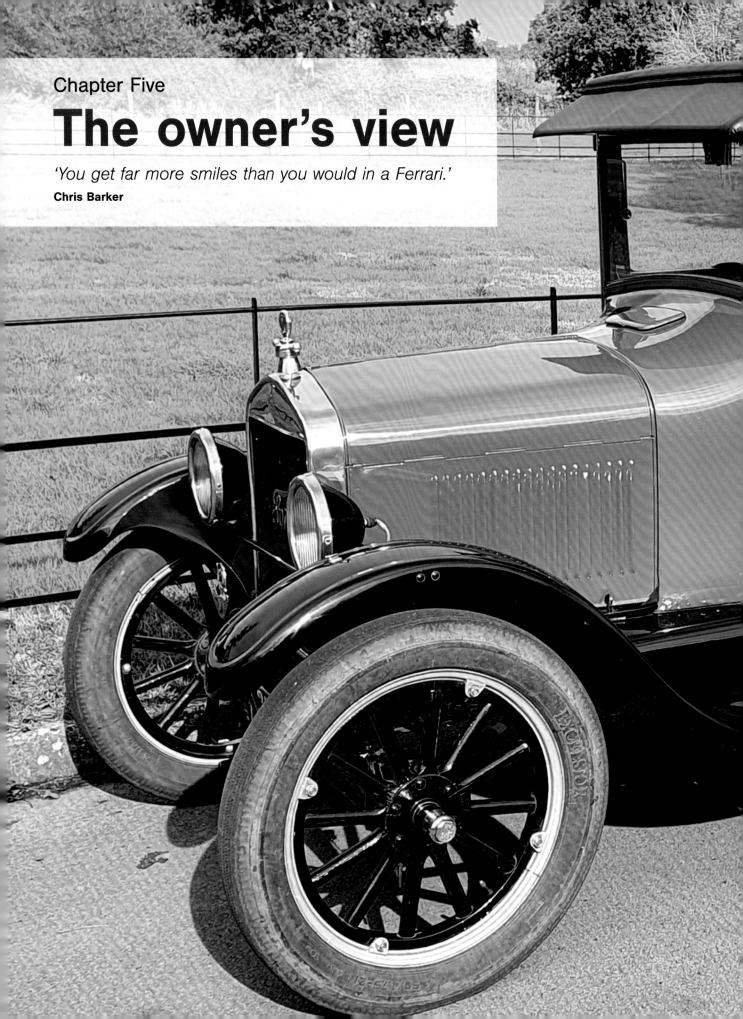

Chapter Five

The owner's view

'You get far more smiles than you would in a Ferrari.'
Chris Barker

**Chris Barker with his
1926 'Improved' Coupé.**
(Chris Barker Collection)

Chris Barker – 1926 'Improved' Coupé

'I was one of the last intake of Rootes student apprentices in 1969 because I studied automotive engineering at Loughborough University and that was a sandwich course. It was Rootes when I went there and then became Chrysler UK, and the week after I graduated, I swapped the Hillman Imp I had for a Sunbeam Alpine, which I still have. Over the years I would go to car shows and see cars like a Rover P5B Coupé or a Jowet Javelin or an E-type fixed-head and think, "They're quite nice." The sort of things you look at but don't do anything about.

'Then in 2000, I happened to be at the National Motor Museum at Beaulieu when the Model T Register turned up with 20 or 30

Model Ts. I walked round and thought, "These are different." The thing about all the other cars I'd considered buying was, "What do you do with them?" I'd got the Sunbeam Alpine, which is a very practical, sensible car. I like driving it, it'll just about carry the family, it'll go, it's economical and reliable, it's adequately quick – what would I do with something else that I can't do with that?

'The Model T was totally different. It was also interesting as a piece of machinery, and a seed was sown. I looked at Neil Tuckett's website off and on, and two years later I found the one I've got now. Unlike most people who look for a Model T, I liked the later Coupés. They are lower than earlier open cars which can't get under an up-and-over garage door with the hood up. You can imagine driving home in the rain, wanting to

(Chris Barker Collection)

put the car away and you've got to put the roof down first. The '26 Coupé will fit under, with a little bit to spare. I've never wanted another one, or a second. There are people in the Model T Register who have two, or three, or even 13 Model Ts at home.

'My car is an "Improved" Coupé – not a Doctor's Coupé – Ford never used that term. "Improved" cars were post-September 1925, with new bodies, nickel radiator shell, scuttle fuel tanks (more gravity), a wider brake drum and bigger emergency brakes. It's November 1926, about 14.5 millionth out of 15 million.

'When I bought it, I was pleasantly surprised to find that, not only did I have an interesting piece of machinery (and as an engineer I like machinery) but also a very important part of social and industrial history. You've got all this which you wouldn't find with something else, and you've also got a club.

'To buy a Model T you've got to be slightly off-beam to say the least, haven't you? Owners tend to be "interesting". It's not the same people who buy an A35 or a Humber Hawk. And furthermore, the club doesn't do parking and polishing, it does driving. Membership of the Register has really enriched our lives

'The furthest I've done in a day from home is Chester, which is about 200 miles. 100 miles a day is fine, 200 is probably as much as you'd want to do, but we got there about four o'clock, so if we'd had to do another 30–40 miles, it wouldn't have been the end of the world. From Chester we went on to Malham Tarn, and then to Kirby Lonsdale, and then in one day we did Penrith and back over Kirkstone Pass. Neil Tuckett once drove from Buckinghamshire to Fort William in one go – 17 hours I think it took him.

'The ride's quite reasonable, though a bit noisy. The open cars are very different to the closed ones. The open ones have much more of a veteran car feel about them. You hear the engine chuffing – the same noise you get as they go past, as opposed to the noise you get inside.

'Generally, other road users react very well. You get far more smiles than you would in a Ferrari. I've never had, touch wood, an obviously adverse reaction. Occasionally what does happen is that you're going along at a speed you can do (about 35mph/56kph), and you get one or two cars behind you. Not a lot of

---

THE MODEL T REGISTER

The Model T Register of Great Britain was founded in 1960 by the late Charles Pearce with the aim of encouraging the preservation and use of early Ford vehicles from 1903–27. With a thriving membership of over 450 in Britain and overseas, the club is run entirely by enthusiasts on a voluntary basis with the purpose of organising social events, including a varied calendar of touring rallies, and providing services such as historical research, supply of new and used spare parts, technical information and books for its membership.

'Its origins are in the late fifties, when a few people began to find Model Ts and put them back together,' explains club archivist Chris Barker. 'Somewhere along the line, Lord Montagu got involved and he encouraged this small band to start a club, which they did in 1960. The first meeting was held at Beaulieu and in 2010 we had a 50th anniversary meeting, also at Beaulieu with the same Lord Montagu. People continued to use these cars because you can still find whatever it is you need. If you want to drive a hundred-year-old car and you can't afford a Silver Ghost, then the Model T is the practical alternative. Unfortunately, our 60th anniversary event has had to be postponed for two years because of the Coronavirus.

'We import spares directly from one or two of the American suppliers and sell them to members,' he continues. 'We can only sell to members for tax reasons and to encourage people to join, and over the year the typical turnover is about £40,000 in new spares. I think we have some used crankshafts, but that's all; everything else is brand new. One big event is the annual Autojumble. The spares are all there, at 10% off that day, and we hold an auction, where there's a mixture of stuff that members bring along. The Register also brings containers of old stock and used spares, some of them imported from the USA where Ford parts are cheaper and more plentiful.

'We're fortunate to have three main specialists in the UK – for those unwilling or unable to work on their cars.'

---

people nowadays do overtaking, except on dual carriageways and motorways, so although you pull over and make room for them, and there are opportunities, they don't pass. Then on a blind bend there'll be someone that comes past the lot and nearly hits somebody coming the other way.

'But you try not to get in people's way, and if we do our tours and you've got 30 cars, we try not to be in a convoy. Two or three is maximum. We did a tour that started at Tiverton in Devon and went to Falmouth, and we deliberately set out in threes so that if somebody had a problem, there were two other people, but we didn't have more than three.'

Neil Tuckett – A range of Model Ts from 1911 Tourer to late 1927, including Commercials and Racers

'My great uncle, John Brazil, was a butcher in Buckinghamshire and in 1924 he bought a van from new, and we still have it. He repainted it in the fifties for publicity for the business – sausages and pies – and he used to do the London to Brighton commercial vehicle run in it. In 1978 he said he wanted to do the London to Brighton again, so we entered the commercial run that year. I learnt to drive it in a field at Amersham and then we trailered it down to Hyde Park and did the London to Brighton. The poor old thing was so tired, but we did get down there. It was "a guinea a minute" is how I'd put it. I was a young fitter and he said "you'd better mend it", so that started me off.

'That was 1978, so I used to look after that, and when he died some years later, he left it to me to continue using it. Meanwhile, in 1981 I bought another car with my brother, because there was one for sale in Aylesbury. At that time, spares were found through *Exchange & Mart* and word of mouth, and there were a few

people around the country who were eccentric enthusiasts, who you'd ring up and they would have spares. That's how we started.

'My 1911, that's my old workhorse and is used pretty much daily. I bought it off the second owners. I'm going up to Norway and the Arctic Circle with it this year, a 2,000-mile run. I've been threatening to do it for years and this is the year. That's why the radiator is off. It wasn't leaking but things were falling off it.' [Since being interviewed early in 2020, Neil's plans for the Arctic Circle trip were put on indefinite hold due to Covid-19. He still intends to undertake it one day, though.]

'Other road users are generally courteous and polite, and for some reason, a Model T always turns the head. I have no idea why, but everyone seems to know that it's a Model T Ford, and that must be to do with the old black-and-white films, Charlie Chaplin, and all those sorts of things. That must be part of it, because we're past the generation that remember them on the road. Most antique cars people buy because they remember them as a kid, or grandad had them or whatever, but the Model T is past that. There's something quirky about it and I can't actually put my finger on what it is.

'If you put a tatty old Model T alongside a brand-new Rolls-Royce, at the end of the day, the crowds are all round the Model T and the Rolls-Royce hasn't had a look in. It doesn't make sense. Everyone should look at the Rolls first and then the tatty old Model T, but it's the other way round. There's no really good reason but one probably is that the Model T is classless. It was a cheap vehicle in its time, and today anyone from a student to a multi-millionaire can own one, and anyone in between.

'It's not for the rich, it's not for the poor. It doesn't matter. With a Bentley or a Rolls-Royce, it's definitely a class of people who own it, but Model Ts seem to cover the whole spectrum. There's no rhyme or reason for it. Everyone has their own reason for owning one. Certainly, it's quirky and definitely a head turner, but then I'm biased.

'I've got quite a few that are working as commercial vehicles for wedding hire. I've got one hearse that works full time, and one or two other vans that are used for publicity purposes. There is no reason why they couldn't be used commercially or practically today, but tend not to, because often there's things like Fleur de Lys, the Transit-based lookalikes, that are more likely to be used for pure practical purposes. But I haven't got a problem driving some of my cars any distance if that's required. The practicalities of timing are not as good, since you're doing 30mph (48kph) all day, whereas a modern car can do 60mph (97kph). But in reality, the average speed of a modern car would only be around 38mph (61kph), and my average speed's probably 30mph (48kph) because I'm at the front of the traffic, so if we set off at the same time, I wouldn't be that far behind.

'Some of these Model Ts, I've no idea what mileage they've done. One of them has been round the clock three times, and that's a 10,000-mile clock so 30,000. I'm heading for 40,000 and that's what I know, and certainly there are records of cars doing two or three hundred thousand at the time.'

Richard Skinner – 1916 'Dakota Katy' and 1921 Open four-seater

'My parents met through vintage cars and they got married in a 1915 Model T. I went on my first London to Brighton run when I was just a few weeks old. I think there was a picture in the *Daily Mail* of my mother wringing out terry nappies at the side of the road, so I was involved with old cars from day one and am still loving it to this day!

'We always had vintage cars and between Dad and myself we have had well over a hundred Model Ts, so it really has been a major part of our lives. As well as vintage cars I have had many motorbikes and all sorts of other crazy machinery. So it's not just Model Ts but it's fair to say that Model Ts have been a central focus of my interests. Sadly, we lost Dad a few years ago, but his legacy certainly lives on.

'Model T Fords are an iconic, quirky and interesting car. It was such an amazing development that Henry Ford came up with. When you think that all the manufacturers during that particular era of motoring history were all

over the place. They were all trying to come up with a common design, and they were all keeping their doors and design rooms shut while coming up with their own versions. Then for Ford to have the initiative to go and get the best structural engineer, the best stress engineer, the best this, the best that, and they all just knuckled down and in October 1908 they came up with the most amazing design. I think it is just such a remarkable story, and I don't think it's been repeated through the history of motoring.

The car itself is so amazing. When you think 15 million were made over a period of 19 years in the early part of the development of cars,

for that design to have lasted right up to the end of the twenties, I think is pretty remarkable. When you get into the cars, you understand why they're made of vanadium steel, and are all three-point mounted so they can't break. They were designed to take over from the horse and cart and did so very successfully for nearly 20 years. They are a phenomenally interesting design of car, very quirky to drive and I think they are the epitome of a vintage car. If a child sat down and did a pictorial representation of a vintage car it's probably going to look like a Model T.

'I was eight when I drove my first Model T, so I had two cushions behind me and Dad put wooden extensions on the pedals. Luckily, we had quite a nice big garden and he taught me to drive in the same car that they got married in, which, looking back, was really special. I used to sit and read all of Dad's Floyd Clymer books on Model Ts and so it was all pretty familiar. Dad said it was really weird, I just got in it and sort of knew what to do because I'd soaked it up like a child's brain does. I just couldn't reach the pedals yet!

'I've got a 1916, which is called Dakota Katy, which I restored for *Practical Classics* magazine. I actually bought it for spare parts and it only cost me about $1,100. I just thought it was good for spares, but Danny Hopkins, the editor of *Practical Classics*, came to visit to do an

article on the business and said, "That's about as bad as a Model T gets." The whole thing had collapsed on itself coming over from North Dakota. We both agreed it would be a really interesting project for *Practical Classics* readers to read about the restoration of the car from the sorry state she was to the beautiful example she is today. We also felt it would be a good way to promote the Model T to a wider audience. So now we have Dakota Katy restored to her former glory after such a long time, as well as my late Dad's 1921, which is also an open four-seater Tourer.'

Ian Morgan – 1913 Open Tourer

'**M**y grandad had one originally, a 1913 or '14 Tourer, the first time round when they were new. I've always been a complete and utter petrolhead, even from being four years old, and as a child I can remember being plonked on a tractor and driving round and round a field on this little grey Fergy. I used to love listening to my grandad telling me all about the Model T and I could never understand the pedal arrangement, but I was always intrigued by them.

'I lived down in Dorset but moved up to the Midlands in the 1990s for work, and said to my wife "I'm going to buy a Model T", and she says, "Yeah, you find one, go and get one." This

RIGHT Ian Morgan's 1913 Open Tourer converted to British army specification, complete with bullet screen.
(Ian Morgan collection)

was in the days before the internet, and little did we realise but we lived about 15 miles from Neil Tuckett, and of course I went and met him, and that was it. So that's how it started. From then, it's gone mad really – First World War lorries, a steamroller and Christ knows what, so I'm a complete and utter nutter really.

'Originally, I started off with a nice restored 1926 Canadian Open Tourer, which was all nice and shiny and bright. I rebuilt the engine and mechanically did it all. Cosmetically, it all looked quite nice, as if it had come out of a museum, but then when I was at Neil's he brought in a 1913 very dilapidated, what would have been an Open Tourer but that had been cut down in the '20s into a pickup. It had been run until the late '30s, thrown in a barn, and there it had stayed. I just fell in love with it. I got it running and kept it really tatty and battered and sold the '26. I just don't do shiny really.

'And we've done thousands of miles with that. So that's the 1913, which would have been an Open Tourer, but because it's a '13 you can take the rear section of the body off with four bolts, and what they used to do was then put on a little wooden frame, a pickup, and use it all week, and then take that off, put the seats back in and go off to the church on Sunday.

'It's an incredible thing. The spark plug leads, which came with it from America, are made of barbed wire and are still on it, all the oil lamps work, the gas lamps work – we go night driving with it on carbide. We take it across muddy fields and because we're interested in First World War stuff, I've also got genuine First World War lorries which we've been rebuilding. Back in 2014, at the Dorset Steam Fair, we did a road parade, a convoy of Model Ts, because the British army had thousands of them running around, either as cars or pickups or with little Vickers guns on the back. We quickly painted it, took the screen off and put a bullet screen on it. We had a replica made. It's absolutely ridiculous, though, because if the bullet hits it, it will just come straight up and hit you.

'The plan was for it to stay like that just for that run. All the paint underneath is original and I thought "I can't paint over that", so I got rubberised paint, which will then come off, put that on and greened it over. It's done so much now, we've been to the Somme with it, it's been

to the Shuttleworth Collection, it's been to Ypres twice for the Remembrance days, the Western Front, we did Thiepval with the Battle of the Somme and ended up in *The Times* newspaper, so it's going to end up staying as it is. All it does is depicts what they had. But it's an incredible thing – it rattles, it smokes, all the floorboards are original and your feet go half through them, but it's the most incredible testament to Henry Ford that actually it still keeps going.

'We drive it to events when we can, but a lot of it is the time issues. Last November, we decided we wanted to drive the Liberty lorry to Belgium so we got it on a modern transporter to the tunnel and then we took that one and the "T" off and we drove them through the tunnel, into France, through to Belgium, and down to Ypres, so they do do some miles.

'The little '13 really flies around all over the place, and because it's been left for five years as it is, it's got muddier and dirtier. We've put it through real thick mud, but I won't clean it and people just love it as it is. It wouldn't have been shiny, they would have just used the thing to death. Underneath I still check it for oil and do this and that, but on the surface you'd think it was never touched. I know everyone to their own, but the fact that there's probably too many vehicles here, I don't have time either but they all get a bit of something done. I'm very much, just go and use them.

'I've also got a 1926 absolutely original grain truck. A friend of mine bought it, again from Neil Tuckett, probably 15 years ago. It came in from

ABOVE Rubberised paint, and mud, cover highly original paintwork on Ian Morgan's 1913 army-spec Open Tourer. *(Ian Morgan collection)*

Kansas I think, and hadn't been run for years. It has never been touched and even though it's 1926, it's one of the basic ones. It's got no battery or ignition, it's all magneto, no starter, no dynamo, still magneto lights, so like 1915 spec really. We got it running but he didn't do a lot with it and a couple of years ago he was going to get rid of it, and I decided to buy it because it's so original. I've put new tyres on it and it's got an auxiliary Jumbo three-speed gearbox in it, which was totally knackered, so I managed to rebuild one out of another one that Neil had. The three-speed auxiliary box is quite nice because standard speed on a TT truck is 18mph (29kph) or something ridiculous, whereas with the Jumbo gearbox, which Neil Tuckett rebuilt from two 'boxes for me, you can quite comfortably get up to 25, 26, 27mph-ish (40–43kph), which in the day was more than adequate. We're very lucky that it's still got the original grain body on it and the wood is perfect. All I do is creosote it and oil it.

'It's the most incredible old thing. We've got five or six acres down the bottom of our village, and I went down there and cut a load of logs. It probably had a tonne and a half, two tonnes of logs in it and I just use it. I went off to the agricultural seed merchants last year and went and got a tonne of fertiliser in it, and people said, "You can't put it on there" – "Why not?" It

went out at 25mph (40kph) and it came back at 25mph. So it gets used, that's the thing. I absolutely use them.

'I was lucky in that it only took me ten minutes or a quarter of an hour to learn to drive one when I started out. Probably because I'd read that many books and I am very mechanically minded. That's not to say the very first time we went out on a Neil Tuckett April Fools' Run in about 1997, in the nice shiny 1926 Model T, which I was very proud of, I did the normal thing. You come up to a junction in second gear, I pushed my foot down on the pedal to find neutral, that's all good, about to get going and suddenly my wife says, "There's a car coming." So what did I do? Hit the pedal to the floor because you do with a clutch. I hit first gear and pulled straight out in front of the car. I never did it again! I think we all do that. Everyone has a close one, once. I think if you throw the concept of what we drive today away and actually get into it completely fresh and for what it is, they're incredibly easy. They are so simple. The trouble is, we all go, "Where's my three pedals? Where's my gearstick? What do you mean that's not a clutch pedal!" That's the bit that confuses us.

'We've had so much fun. My daughter went on her first Model T run at five weeks old in the back in a Moses basket, and went to her

RIGHT Ian Morgan's highly original 1926 Ford TT grain truck, still used today.
(Ian Morgan collection)

Christening in it, literally thrown in a basket in the back. We've got a tractor my great uncle bought new in 1941, and the Model T, and my daughter, who's now 14, said to me, "Dad, as and when the time comes that you want to sell everything or whatever, those are the only two you can't sell." So I know the Model T will stay in the family long after I'm dead and gone.'

Richard Rimmer – 1925 Tourer

'**M**y interest was piqued quite a few years ago by a friend who had a little Austin 7 Ruby, but when I came to look for something myself, an Austin's a bit on the small side for someone who's six-foot-plus tall. I had always imagined Model Ts being quite an expensive car for some reason, you have this image that they're going to cost you £30–40,000, but that's not the case. So partly it was the affordability, because they are pretty inexpensive for a hundred-year-old car, but the other thing was that I wanted a car I could actually use and not worry that if I broke it,

it was going to be off the road while I was having parts specially made at huge cost. I didn't want something where when you break a front hub or something you've got to go to an engineering firm and have them made.

'The T is so well-catered for with replacement parts, both new and used. With 15½ million made, there's always used parts around, but the wear and tear items are reproduced, thanks to the fact that there's quite a few of them still in use in the States, so we're very lucky.

'The one that started it for me was a 1925 Tourer. That's the first one we bought and that kicked everything off. It's very much a run-of-the-mill, black radiator, open top car. We particularly wanted an open top four-seater, so we could share it with friends and family, which is what we've done ever since. We bought that from a Model T specialist in America and shipped it back. It's had a fair bit of work since, mechanically, but I've left it cosmetically as it was because I don't want something so pristine that I'm scared to use it.

'In a day we probably do 120–130 miles

ABOVE Richard Rimmer's 1925 Model T Tourer. *(Richard Rimmer collection)*

(190–210km), but we've taken it to France on a trailer for two rallies with friends and then done a few hundred miles over the course of a three- or four-day period. We've driven up to London from Oxfordshire to see the start of the London to Brighton run, leaving home at four o'clock in the morning. Six-volt headlights are little more than candles, so you can only see six foot in front of the car! We stay off the main roads as much as possible and arrive at Hyde Park for probably around seven, seven-thirty in the morning. We watch all the veteran cars leave and then we stop at the Ace Café for breakfast on the way home, which is always a nice venue to stop at, and then trundle back home at our own pace.

'We've been lucky enough to do the run itself since then in a different car. That came about as a result of meeting someone who owned a

Model T, but who also owned a couple of very early Fords as well. It went from "Well, if you're coming up to London anyway in the Model T, why don't you join us for a run as passengers?", to then three years on the trot saying "Well, would you like to drive the car?" It takes a bit of building up of trust with a car that's worth a hundred plus thousand for someone to say, "There you go, you drive it," but that's the stage

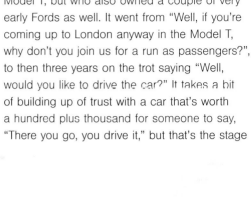

we've got to. We're very lucky from that point of view and I do trade work on the car for the opportunity, and we obviously pay our way, but having that opportunity in the first place and being trusted is a bit special. We've got to meet people in America as a result of doing that, they've brought their early Fords over and it's all a nice social community.

'Apart from that we do events like Kop Hill, where we meet up with friends and family and we can give them a run up the hill. I always say to them, "It's one of the slowest runs up the hill you're going to get," but it's just being involved in some of these things that makes you feel a little bit special, even though the cars are fairly plentiful.

'We tend to cruise at around 35mph (56kph). You can do more but you don't want to be rushing around. The cars are capable of 40mph (64kph) plus, but it isn't kind on them to run flat out. They each have their "happy spot" that they'll run at. If we're doing rallies we haven't got the time to drive to and from them as well as taking part in the event. It's fine if you're retired and you've got plenty of time, but when you're working it's not practical to do that.

'Model Ts tend to be quite a feel-good car, so generally other road users are quite tolerant of us. You get smiles and waves most of the time but, as with any slow-moving vehicle, you'll always get someone who's in a rush. They want to get past you and the worst thing is when they rush past and then hit the brakes in front of you. You can anticipate what you can see but if someone catches you out like that, it can be a bit awkward and unpleasant.

'It's quite incredible how versatile a vehicle the Model T has been, from getting the typical farmer mobile in the States on unmade roads, to being converted to things that competed at Indianapolis and goodness knows where else, and even grass roots level at the "Pig n Ford" races. People are still doing similar things today, in that they're buying a chassis or building a chassis up and making their own Speedster bodies. You can convert it to what you want. People build truck bodies and van bodies and all sorts. It's just the usability and the feel-good side of it that always comes back to me. They do make people smile. I just think they're a nice, friendly car really.'

After building the massive '999' race car in 1902, Henry Ford was reluctant to drive it himself. Instead, he hired bicycle racer Barney Oldfield, who went on to score a number of victories in the car. *(Alamy)*

Chapter Six

Competition history

Henry Ford had recognised the publicity value of using his cars in competition at an early stage. In 1901 he challenged Alexander Winton, founder of the Winton Motor Carriage Company, to a ten-lap race on a one-mile oval at the Detroit Driving Club, Grosse Pointe, Michigan. Winton took an early lead but after seven laps his engine failed, leaving Ford to coast to victory in 'Sweepstakes', a 26hp racing car of his own design, at an average speed of 45mph (72kph).

The following year he built '999', which consisted merely of the bare essentials – chassis, engine, wheels and controls – and hired bicycle racer Barney Oldfield to drive it. In October 1902 he won the five-mile Manufacturers' Challenge Cup at Grosse Pointe, beating Winton, and going on to score a number of other victories in the bright red car.

Another car, built at the same time as '999' and to the same specification, was named 'Arrow' and painted yellow. Sadly, in September 1903, it crashed during a race, killing the driver, Frank Day. Ford repaired the car, which he

confusingly renamed '999', as the original had by now been retired, and on 12 January 1904, he and his riding mechanic, Ed 'Spider' Huff, set a world land speed record of 91.37mph (146.9kph) on a frozen Lake St Clair, northeast of Detroit. This helped to raise the profile of the Ford Motor Company no end.

In 1907, Ford built '666', which proved less successful. Using the engine from the Model K, it was built to break the one-mile track record at the Michigan State Fair. A right tyre failed causing Frank Kulick to crash heavily, leaving him with a permanent limp. The car was never raced again. According to the Michigan Motor Sports Hall of Fame website, Frank Kulick was one of the first five employees of the Ford Motor Company and became the number one factory racing driver, a position he held for a decade.

Ford decided that there was more publicity to be gained in racing a car that the public could buy for themselves than those built specifically for racing, and so he prepared two Model Ts to take part in the 1909 Ocean to Ocean Automobile Endurance Contest, also

ABOVE Ford entered
two Model Ts in the
Ocean to Ocean race
in 1909. Frank Kulick
and H.P. Harper drove
one car, with Bert Scott
and Jimmy Smith in
the other. The cars are
shown near the starting
line in New York.
(Ford Images)

RIGHT Bert Scott and
Jimmy Smith shared
the No. 2 Model T entry
in the 1909 Ocean to
Ocean race.
(Ford Images)

known as the Transcontinental Contest for the Guggenheim Trophy. This was run from New York to Seattle, with the first car leaving New York on 1 June 1909 and arriving on 23 June. It was held in conjunction with the Yukon-Pacific Exposition, the world's fair at Seattle, which also began on 1 June.

Both Model Ts were four-cylinder 20hp, 1,200lb (544kg) models, and Ford was allocated the numbers one and two as it was the first manufacturer to enter. Car No. 1 was driven by Frank Kulick and H.P. Harper and No. 2 by Bert Scott and Jimmy Smith.

Recounting the event in *The Story of the Race*, published by the Ford Motor Company, one of the drivers of Ford No. 1, though not identified, wrote: 'Every day we wore rubber coats and hip boots and pushed through mile after mile of mud. The monotony of this was frequently varied by having to ford a stream where the unusual rainfall had washed away the bridge. Often these swollen streams had beds

of quicksand and the car striking them would instantly sink until the body resting on the sand prevented further settling. Then we thanked our lucky stars that we of the Ford crews were driving light cars. Where a heavy car had to resort to horses and a block and tackle, the two men in each Ford car could pick up their car, place the wheels on planks and proceed along.'

The race was won by the No. 2 Ford, driven by Scott and Smith, which covered the 4,106 miles in 20 days and 52 minutes, 17 hours ahead of the second-placed car, a Shawmut. The No. 1 Ford lost time and finished third. Only much later was it discovered that the winning Ford had had its engine replaced part way through the event, thereby disqualifying it. By then, Ford had enjoyed the publicity surrounding the event anyway. The race was re-enacted in 2009 with 35 Model T Fords taking part.

Between 1910 and 1913, Frank Kulick raced a highly modified Model T, entered by the Ford Motor Company, at a number of events.

On 17 February 1912, he reached 107.8mph (173.5kph) on the frozen Lake St Clair, near Detroit. Ford ended official participation in competition in 1913, as by then it was too busy making and selling the cars and deemed the extra publicity unnecessary.

However, Ford didn't need to go racing himself, as many Model T owners were already doing it for him, using their machines as the basis for a number of heavily modified stock cars, which they raced on small, dirt, oval tracks. Many of these featured a special cylinder head made by the Frontenac company, which had been formed by the Chevrolet brothers, Louis and Arthur, in 1916. It was named after Comte de Frontenac, the 17th-century governor of France's North American colonies, in order to disguise the fact that the Chevrolets were making components for other manufacturers' cars. The company made cylinder heads and valve assemblies for Model T dirt track racers, which

tripled the available power. They proved highly successful and were still in use in the 1940s.

The Frontenac Ford, or 'Fronty' as it was known, was an overhead valve conversion for the 2.9-litre (177-cu in) Ford engine, although a special version was made for the 2.0-litre (122-cu in) engine in order to conform with the rules for the Indianapolis 500. Around 10,000 Frontenac cylinder heads of various types were made and the original featured a single inlet port with triple exhaust ports in a crossflow design. The 'R' was for race cars, the 'S' for road-going Speedsters, and the 'T' version for touring cars and trucks. The later 'S-R' included two intake ports and provision for spark plugs on either side of the head. In 1924 the company developed the 'D-O' (or double overhead) which featured 16 valves, two inlet and exhaust per cylinder, and two chain-driven camshafts. The crossflow design had separate inlet and exhaust ports for each cylinder, with spark plugs located in the top of the head.

BELOW Frank Kulick driving his Ford at the 1910 Point Breeze racetrack in Philadelphia.
(Detroit Public Library)

Indianapolis 500

Frontenacs had been regular runners at the Indianapolis 500 from 1916 onwards, with the Chevrolet brothers driving their own Frontenac-engined Frontenacs. That year both Louis and Arthur retired, but in 1919, the next time the event was run, Louis and Gaston finished seventh and tenth respectively. The following year Gaston drove to overall victory, with Tommy Milton repeating the success in 1921 when the field included a total of six Frontenac-Frontenacs.

The first appearance of a Model T-Fronty-Ford at Indianapolis was in 1922, when Jack Curtner drove one to 14th place. In the same year, C. Glenn Howard, in another Model T-Fronty-Ford entered by the Chevrolet brothers, was classified 18th, despite retiring – apparently with a broken left front wheel – after 163 of the 200 laps.

In 1923, Indianapolis car dealer Barber-Warnock entered a single Model T-Fronty-Ford for L.L. Corum, which finished a highly respectable fifth. Inspired by this success, the following year they entered three such cars, named the Barber-Warnock Specials. One was fitted with the 'D-O' cylinder head, while the other two featured the earlier 'S-R' version. All three cars finished the race. Car #26 was driven by Bill Hunt, who started 19th and finished 14th. Car #27 was driven by Fred Harder, who started 22nd and finished 17th, while car #28 was driven by Alfred Moss, father of Stirling, who started 20th and finished 16th. Four other privately entered Frontenac-Fords failed to qualify for the race.

BELOW **This Ford T-Frontenac, or 'Fronty-Ford', was driven at the 1922 Indianapolis 500 by C. Glenn Howard and classified 18th, despite retiring.** *(Alamy)*

ALFRED MOSS

Alfred Moss was a successful London dentist and amateur racing driver who, aged 27, went to Indianapolis in 1924 on the pretext of studying advanced dental practice but in reality to be able to compete in the 500-mile race. Moss had already started racing in 1921 at the wheel of an AV Bicar in the Essex Motor Club Winter Trial through Epping Forest. In 1923 he drove a Crouch-Anzani at Brooklands with some success.

Having enrolled at the Indianapolis Dental College, he lined up for the start of that year's Indy 500 at the wheel of a Model T-based Frontenac Ford, finishing a respectable 16th. After spending a few months competing on dirt tracks in the US, he returned to England in 1925, building himself a Frontenac Ford from a Model T chassis and racing it at Brooklands that August Bank Holiday in the Short Handicap event.

With his dental business growing, he retired from racing, only to later support the career of his son Stirling, who was born in 1929.

BELOW Stirling Moss sits in a Ford Frontenac, similar to that driven by his father, Alfred, at the 1924 Indianapolis 500, at Goodwood Festival of Speed in 2003. *(Motorsport Images)*

ABOVE Barber-Warnock Special at the Coronado Speed Festival in California in October 2007. *(Alamy)*

RIGHT Henry Ford poses in the No. 27 Barber-Warnock Frontenac Ford at the Indianapolis 500 in 1924. Behind him can be seen Louis Chevrolet (with thick moustache), Barney Oldfield (with cigar) and Edsel Ford (in plaid overcoat). The car, which was driven by Fred Harder, finished 17th. *(Getty Images)*

Frontenac-Fords appeared at the Indy 500 the following two years as well, but without any success.

Neil Tuckett owns a Frontenac Ford, although he is still researching its full provenance. 'I think my car is the forerunner of the Barber-Warnock Specials,' he says. 'It was not in that 1924 Indy 500 race, as far as I can ascertain. I believe it's a prototype because everything is pretty similar,

RIGHT A Ford
Frontenac also
competed in Britain at
the Lewes Speed Trials
on 19 September 1931.
(NMM)

other than the front axle is more standard and they'd gone to a tubular axle. Also, this one was only running four spark plugs and Alfred Moss's and the others were running eight. I think it was a factory build at a stage slightly before the others.

'The Frontenac is a full race car,' he explains. 'The Chevrolet brothers built an overhead valve head to go on a Dodge engine. They quickly realised if they changed it to go on a Model T Ford engine, there were three million potential customers out there. That's what they did and they went racing. It's a Model T chassis, Model T block, Model T back and front axle, it's just the head that's different. Mine has the S-R head, which developed into having a single overhead cam and then in 1927 went to a double overhead cam. So you can see the stages. Mine seems to fit in just prior to that race [1924 Indy 500] and I reckon it was a factory build as an experimental prototype and then it got sold on. It didn't race in that Indy 500, and where it raced I currently have little information. It might

have been one of the ones which was entered but didn't qualify.

'A guy in Australia recognised it and he's confirmed that it's genuine factory-built and which model it was. He said that the body is specifically 1923. Someone knows about it and it'll come to light eventually. It could have been one of the unqualified ones. It's so specific, there are certain things about it that just jump at you.

'They were selling them out of the back door of the factory at $2,500, which was a lot of money. Or you buy them in bits, which is what a lot of the guys like John Gerber did. They were building them out of their own garages, which was a great system, really.

'I have fun with it and run it anywhere and everywhere, including Pendine Sands. I originally sold it 20 years ago as a commission sale and I bought it back about two years ago. It had not moved one inch in 20 years and was still in the garage where I put it. So I had to buy it back.'

Le Mans 24-Hours

Aheavily modified version of the Model T, known as the Ford-Montier, was entered for the Le Mans 24 Hours from 1923–25, by Parisian Ford dealer, Charles Montier, and his brother-in-law, Albert Ouriou.

The chassis had been lowered by 170mm by using steel triangulations to support the transverse springs, front and rear, and the car featured new hubs with Rudge wire wheels, a new radiator and revised bodywork. Montier designed his own cylinder head for the engine with high-lift, wide overhead valves, aluminium alloy pistons and an uprated Solex carburettor. A Ruckstall rear-axle conversion provided an extra two gears and the brakes were uprated with a Perrot-style system.

The pair finished 14th in 1923 but a stone punctured the oil tank the following year, forcing them to retire. In 1924 a loose wheel also forced the pair into retirement but the same year, the Ford-Montier won its class in four hill climbs.

Europe

A Google search reveals that on 11 September 1926 at Bari in Italy, Battista Suglia finished fourth driving a Model T Ford in a race won by Guido Casale in a Lancia Lambda, while on 3 November 1929 in the Coppa di Crollalanza, also at Bari, Suglia finished fifth behind Enrico Zalar in another Model T, the race being won by the OM of Archimede Rosa. In the 1930 running of the Coppa di Crollalanza on 20 September, Nella de Facendis finished third in a Model T, the winner being Ernesto Abbaticola driving an Alfa Romeo 1500.

Model Ts were also used for ice racing in Sweden. 'They put spiked wheels on them and off they went,' comments Neil Tuckett, 'and also beach racing in New Zealand.'

The Golden Ford

The Golden Ford was a 1911 racer that was built in Newcastle by the firm of George and Jobling, which in 1904 had taken over the premises previously used by Robert Stephenson & Co to build the revolutionary Rocket steam engine. It was owned and raced by Arthur Edward George, who was an international cyclist and the first man to fly a mile in Britain. On August Bank Holiday Monday 1912, he won the All-Ford Brooklands Challenge driving the car, a feat witnessed by Henry Ford who was watching from the grandstands and who presented him with the winner's cup at the end.

The following year it was fitted with a single-

BELOW Neil Tuckett's Golden Ford.
(Neil Tuckett Collection)

seat, narrow body made of polished brass, hence the name. The car was raced with some success on Saltburn Sands between 1912 and 1914 before being modified for George's daughter to learn to drive. It is another historic Model T which is owned by Neil Tuckett.

'It's an early single-seater race car that was found in a cellar,' he explains. 'It is pretty well stock because they had to run stock pistons, stock back axle and so on. They had a bigger carburettor early on and sometime after the First World War an overhead valve head was put on it. It was never successful after the First World War. It hasn't been lowered but we can run this to about 70mph (112kph) but after 55–60mph (89–96kph), it's quite a handful. On the original skinny wheels, you can hardly handle it after 60mph (96kph). But they soon learnt. They started lowering it and adding wider wheels. But it's historic, it won at Brooklands at the grand speed of 56¾mph (91.3kph).

'I haven't got much history about it but I found some pictures, because the body was missing. We rebuilt that with the *Salvage Squad* [TV programme] and they did some research and found the daughter of the original owner, aged 92. She came to Brooklands to see it when we rebuilt it, and she just walked up to it and said: "Where did you get the body from?" I explained that we rebuilt it, because it was

gone. "Well I know it was gone," she said. "It was in the workshop and was all chopped up in the Second World War by the Italian prisoners of war for making trinket boxes." So there's the answer, that's why the body wasn't there.'

Pig n Ford races

If it isn't difficult enough to master driving a Model T Ford, then driving one while holding a live pig is only going to complicate matters, yet that is exactly what happens at the annual Tillamook County Fair in Oregon, USA. The tradition apparently started in 1925 when a Model T owner spotted a loose pig, caught it and returned it to its owner, holding the squealing animal under one arm. Another story is that it was two local farmers chasing a runaway pig in their Model Ts and thought it was so much fun they would organise a race.

Now, each August at the County Fair, ten competitors run across the track, Le Mans style, scoop up a 20lb pig from a pen, run to their stripped Model Ts and crank the engine with their free hand. They then race around a dirt track for one lap before stopping, turning off the engine, selecting a different pig from the pen and repeating the process for two more laps. The winner is the first one home without dropping his pig on the way.

BELOW **The annual Pig n Ford races at the Tillamook County Fair in Oregon.**
(Linda Freedman)

Chapter Seven
Endless varieties

Farmworkers loading hay onto a Model T Ford truck at a farm in Bedford in June 1922.
(Topical Press Agency/ Getty Images)

ABOVE Rural Free Delivery (RFD) carrier Harold Crabtree of Central Square, New York, used this 1921 Model T Ford with snowmobile attachment. The front wheels were interchangeable with skis and the rear tyres accommodated tank-like treads, allowing the vehicle to move more easily over snow and ice. *(Alamy)*

RIGHT A Red Cross nurse with a new Model T Ford in Bridgeton, Massachusetts, 1916. *(Alamy)*

The uses to which the Model T Ford was put over the years, and the range of body styles attached to the chassis, are far too numerous to cover in their entirety. In addition, aftermarket accessories allowed it to be converted for many applications, including half-track conversions that were used by the military.

During its lifetime, the Model T was adapted to all sorts of uses, particularly in agricultural areas. It could be used as a stationary engine, by removing one of the driven wheels and using a belt and pulley to power a variety of machinery, such as an electric generator, a conveyor belt, threshing machine, saw or water pump.

Delivery van

The first British-built commercial vehicle to emerge from the Trafford Park facility was a delivery van, which was introduced in 1912. It could carry loads of up to 7cwt (356kg) and replaced the horse-drawn cart as a means of making door-to-door deliveries of light loads for businesses such as bakeries, but aftermarket conversions to increase its carrying capacity soon became available (see Ton Truck, below). By 1924, the production of Model T commercials had passed that of cars.

The Ton Truck

The Model TT, or Ton Truck, was based on standard Model T running gear, but incorporated a longer and heavier chassis frame and modified rear axle. It first appeared in July 1917 as just a chassis but from 1924 was available with a factory-produced body. The Ton Truck was only built in response to a number of aftermarket suppliers who started to make conversion kits to allow a standard Model T van or lorry carry heavier loads, as Chris Barker explains.

'About 1913–14 a number of American companies produced conversions – they were

ABOVE **Model T Ford staff car, belonging to the Scottish Fusilier Regiment, pictured at Poperinge, Belgium, 1917.** *(Alamy)*

called extensions,' he says. 'What you got was an extra chassis that slid over the original one and then some means of increasing the load capacity and lowering the gearing. This was done by using different sprockets to lower the gearing and a different set of springs and a dead rear axle to take bigger loads.

'Others put extra springs in and then had reduction gearing in the hubs. These extension kits that came out almost all lengthened the wheelbase as well. They became popular, and Ford, or rather the company, reacted very badly and sent out service bulletins to the dealers, telling them not to have anything to do with these. But then, in 1917, they introduced the Ford Ton Truck, which was almost the same thing except it was done properly, in that it had a longer chassis, slightly heavier side members, a much heavier transverse leaf spring and a worm gear with much lower gearing and heavier rear axle, but front axle and engine and transmission were exactly the same.

'So having said, "No, no you mustn't do it, it

will never work," they decided later, "Maybe it does work, we need to get in on this" – and so they produced the Ton Truck.'

The chassis was extended from 100in to 125in (254cm to 318cm), and the rear axle modified to include a worm drive and crown wheel, rather than a crown wheel and pinion. The TT was slow compared to its competitors, with a top speed of just 20–22mph (32–35kph) with standard gearing. Even with extra gearing, 27–28mph (43–45kph) was the likely top speed, resulting in a number of aftermarket suppliers producing special items such as the Ruckstell twin-speed rear axle or Jumbo gearbox, which provided intermediate gears to assist when climbing steep hills, and accessories to produce more power.

The initial chassis on its own cost $380, and promotional material from 1923 proclaims:

A price so low – a value so great – a utility so necessary that every merchant, manufacturer, contractor, should now own a Ford One-Ton

Truck. Thousands in daily use all over the country, cutting hauling costs, saving time and making money for their owners.

The Ford One-Ton Truck Chassis is steady, dependable and efficient in service. It costs little to operate and maintain. Equipped with pneumatic, non-skid cord rear tires (solid tires optional). Your choice of special gearing $5\frac{1}{6}$ to 1 for speed delivery or the standard gearing of $7\frac{1}{4}$ to 1 for heavy hauling. We can supply a body to suit your needs.

'People did all sorts of things, and then they extended the chassis and then they extended it some more, so you ended up with two-ton trucks,' adds Chris Barker.

Depot Hacks

It wasn't long before independent coachbuilders were also offering a range of body styles to fit the Model T chassis, including the open wooden-bodied, multi-seat Depot Hack, a predecessor of the station wagon or estate car, which was designed to carry a number of passengers and their luggage from a railway station to their hotel.

'In the UK we call them Dixies,' explains Neil Tuckett, 'but in America they call them Depot Hacks. They were quite clever because

you could have three sets of seats for carrying people, or you could have a tailgate, and take one row of seats out and make it into a pickup. You could take the roof off if you wanted it open, you could put sides in with screens or whatever. These were the first of the universal vehicles – SUVs or whatever else you want to call them – and they were quite clever designs.'

Wartime

As a pacifist, Henry Ford had been against America entering the First World War and the use of his cars in combat, but he eventually relented. In 1917 he supported the war effort by making and selling 390,000 rolling chassis and spare parts to the US Army for conversion into ambulances and other vehicles, of which around 15,000 saw service in Europe.

At the outbreak of the war, Model Ts were purchased from Ford dealerships in Britain and France and first appeared as field service ambulances on the front line in 1915. According to Jon Branch in his article 'A Brief History of the Model T Ford – Everything You Need to Know' on silodrome.com, the French army fielded around 11,000 Model Ts for the war effort, while British and Empire forces fielded somewhere between 20–30,000, the vehicles being used in Europe, Africa and the Middle East.

The Trafford Park factory in the UK was turned over to war production and supplied the British government with 30,000 vehicles. Blakes of Liverpool made ambulance bodies (2,645 between 1915 and 1920) while the British army mounted Lewis or Vickers machine guns on the scuttle and used the Model T as a reconnaissance patrol car. It served on the Western Front in France and also as Light Motor Batteries (LAMBYs) during the Western Desert campaign in Egypt and Libya. Colonel T.E. Lawrence (of Arabia) also used one during his time in Mesopotamia.

The Australian Imperial Force's 1st Armoured Car Battery was equipped with Model Ts, armed with a Vickers .303 machine gun mounted on a tripod in the rear of the vehicle, in its campaign against the Senussi in the Sudan and Western Desert.

According to *The Ford in Britain File* by Eric Dymock, Royal Flying Corps Captain Benny

BELOW 1925
Depot Hack.
(Neil Tuckett collection)

ABOVE 1917
Light Patrol Car.
(Neil Tuckett collection)

LEFT 1915 Ford Model
T 'Hucks Starter',
adapted to start
First World War-type
aeroplanes. *(Alamy)*

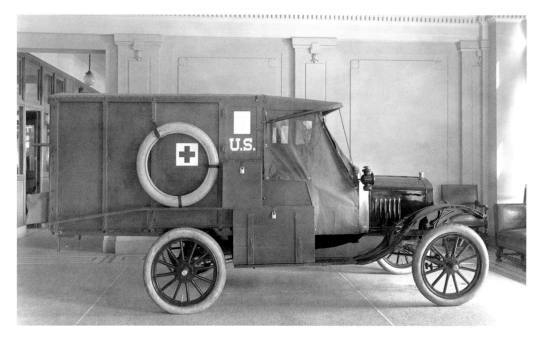

Hucks, a test pilot for the Airco company of Hendon, 'designed a mechanism to start aircraft engines off the Model T's epicyclic transmission. A chain drive from the rear of the gearbox to an overhead shaft spun the propellor, which was a good deal safer than having it swung by a hapless aircraftsman.'

Ambulance

When the United States entered World War I, Ford Motor Company personnel collaborated with the US Surgeon General's Office, as well as drivers who had served on the front lines in France, to design a Model T-based ambulance suited to battlefield conditions. Ford built 5,745 ambulances for the Allied armies during the war, and another 107 for the Red Cross.

The Model T ambulance became a familiar sight on the battlefields since it was able to traverse ground that other vehicles could not, and its light weight (about 1,300lbs/590kg) meant it could be easily pushed if it did get stuck.

Ford Railcars

Perhaps one of the more unusual requests that restorer Neil Tuckett had was from the owner of a private narrow-gauge railway for him to build a Model T Railcar. 'This guy has an 800-metre railway in his garden,' Neil explains, 'with the only Darjeeling locomotive outside India. He rang me one day and said, "I want to build a

Model T train. It takes two hours to steam up my locomotive and I want a Model T so I can turn the key and use it for shunting." So the rail loco guys did the bottom, and we did the top. It's a Model T chassis, they just met in the middle.

'The strange thing is,' he continues, 'when you drive it, there's no steering wheel. A steering column, but no wheel. You go to drive a car without a steering wheel and it's the most strange feeling. And when you go backwards everyone turns round. There's no need to turn round, you just press the pedal, there's nothing behind you.'

In fact, Model T Railcars are nothing new, and have been used with varying success in a number of countries. The author and travel writer Paul Theroux makes reference to a Model T Ford locomotive in his 1975 book, *The Great Railway Bazaar*. While travelling in India, he comes across the following:

This was a white squarish-machine, with the face of a Model T Ford and the body of an old bus. It was mounted low on the narrow-gauge tracks and had the look of a battered limousine. But considering that it was built in 1925 (so the driver assured me), it was in wonderful shape.

India isn't the only country that boasts a Model T Railcar. In New Zealand, in the latter part of the 1920s, two Railcars based on the Ton Truck

chassis operated on the country's national rail network. Designated the NZR RM class, they were designed for use on small, country branch lines and were to be operated by a single person. The engine and transmission were pure Model T Ford with a passenger compartment 11ft by 7ft (3.4 x 2.1m) mounted on the chassis. Unfortunately, they didn't prove a success and were unpopular with passengers, eventually being withdrawn.

In America, a Model T was converted into a crew car for the two-foot gauge Sandy River and Rangeley Lakes Railroad in 1925.

ABOVE In 1925 New Zealand Railways decided to build two lightweight railcars, placed on a one-ton Model T Ford truck chassis, in Wellington's railway workshops. Their construction was part of a national drive by railways to reduce the costs of operating on light traffic lines where there was only a limited number of passengers. The railcars only needed one person to run them, but a train needed at least three. After trials in the North Island, both vehicles were sent to the South Island to run in the Southland area. Rumour has it they were deliberately sent as far away from Wellington as possible. *(Alamy)*

BELOW The first Kent and East Sussex Railway Ford set, as delivered, pictured at Tenterden station. *(K&ESR)*

The development of petrol-powered Railcars, or Railmotors, really began in England, where Col. Holman Stephens, owner of a number of small railways, had begun to look for a cost-effective method of countering competition from road-based transport by adapting a petrol-powered vehicle for use on the rails. At the time, only a few railways in North America and one French manufacturer were attempting similar projects. The other advantage of petrol-powered Railcars was the speed with which they could be brought into operation compared to the lengthy time it took to steam up a conventional locomotive.

Stephens had already experimented with a Wolseley-Siddeley car chassis and, encouraged by this, in 1923 he ordered two sets of Ford railcars for the Kent and East Sussex Railway (K&ESR). These were based upon Model T Ton Truck chassis and built by Edmonds Motors of Thetford with bus bodies supplied by Eton Coachworks of Cringleford. At the time, Stephens said: 'The motive units are the much despised one-ton Fords; we chose this type, as we can always get spares without delay and for no other reason.' One assumes they were despised because they represented competition to the railways.

The Ford Railcars utilised standard Model TT chassis and, to avoid the problem of

reversing, were used in back-to-back pairs, connected using a centre buffer and a draw-pin, despite this meaning that the leading car was always pulling the dead weight of the trailing car. According to *Colonel Stephens and his Railmotors* by Brian Janes and Ross Shimmon, the units were built on the lorry chassis with the standard bonnet and mudguards retained, complete with sidelights, although these soon disappeared. Two headlamps were fitted initially but replaced by a single unit mounted centrally on the roof and a wooden buffer bar attached above and in front of the headlamps. The suspension remained the same and the cars were fitted with pressed steel solid disc flanged wheels. The bodies were made from teak, reinforced with metal plates and sheet metal covering below the waist line and each Railcar could carry 16 passengers on reversible wooden seats.

The driving controls remained the same as on the road-going vehicles and the steering column (minus the steering wheel) with the standard lever controls was retained. The gearbox was the standard two-speed plus reverse epicyclic unit, but later a Supaphord Patented Auxiliary Gear Box was fitted, giving an extra two forward and one reverse gears. According to *Colonel Stephens and his Railmotors*, it is thought that this provided the following ratios: Ford low gear, 20:1; Supaphord low gear, 13.2:1; Ford high gear, 7.2:1; and Supaphord high gear, 4.75:1. The unit also featured a dog clutch, which enabled free-wheeling of the rear unit when being towed.

The petrol tank was originally located underneath the driver's seat, but fumes leaked through the filler cap (not a problem in the open cabs of the road-going TT lorries) and it meant that the seat was mounted so high that some drivers couldn't reach the pedals. The tanks were therefore moved outside and located on the running boards. The lowering of the seat caused the driver to now be sitting much lower than his passengers on a seat that was apparently not attached to the floor.

The light weight and single-axle drive meant that wheel spin could be a problem and so a sand bucket was fitted either side of the driver's seat, with an iron pipe projecting through the floor in front of the rear wheels.

BELOW Driver Nelson Wood is at the controls of the Ford Railcar. Note the absence of the steering wheel but otherwise the driving controls remained the same as on the road-going Model Ts. Taken from a Pathé newsreel of the time. *(K&ESR)*

LEFT View from behind the driver, showing the low driving position and poor visibility with the central pillar directly in front of him. (K&ESR)

The first Ford Railcar came into service on 15 February 1923, with Pathé News deeming the event worthy of filming. Despite initial teething problems, the Railcars proved to be reliable and achieved high daily mileages, running on the K&ESR between Headcorn in Kent and Robertsbridge in Sussex. Capital costs were low and they were simple to use, eliminating the time spent waiting for a steam locomotive to come up to temperature. Petrol consumption was also good. It is interesting to note that apparently 'horse manure for plugging radiators was a vital part of the emergency equipment carried at all times...'.

BELOW The second Kent and East Sussex Railway Ford set is pictured at Headcorn station. The box on the footboard is the petrol tank. (K&ESR)

Encouraged by their success on the K&ESR, Stephens then introduced a further Ford Railcar set on his Shropshire and Montgomeryshire railway in 1923; in this case a three-car set, although the middle, dummy, car was soon removed but found a home on Stephens' Selsey Tramway.

In 1924, a second Ford Railcar set was purchased for the K&ESR, the major difference between this and the first set being that Ford had now adopted the high radiator on the Model T, with a hole to accommodate the starting handle. However, with Stephens having already stated that the reason for using the Fords was the ready availability of spares, it was not long before this had reverted to the previous low black radiators. K&ESR Railcar number

one remained in operation until 1936, while the second set carried on until the following year.

Stephens also commissioned a third Ford Railcar set, which ran on the Selsey Tramway between Selsey and Chichester in West Sussex from 1924 until the line closed in 1935. The main difference between this and the K&ESR Railcars was the use of curved spoke cast steel wheels, instead of pressed steel solid ones.

Clown Car

One of the more unusual Model Ts looked after by Neil Tuckett is the 'Clown Car' or 'Crazy Car', which is believed to have been originally used in the Keystone Cops black-and-white slapstick films between 1912 and

RIGHT Topping up the radiator of the Selsey Tramway set with water from an old petrol can. Note the curved-spoked wheels and method of supporting the wooden buffer bar.
(K&ESR)

1917, and later by the Bertram Mills Circus performer Nicolai Poliakoff, better known as Coco the Clown.

'If you ever went to the circus you would have seen it,' Neil explains. 'It comes in here for a service and we ran it last year at Kop Hill. It's got three generations of gizmos and tricks on it. It's unbelievable when you're working on it because we always find something new that someone's put on there, and some of them are so clever.

'It's not a replica, it's genuine. I remember it as a kid but I didn't associate it as a Model T at the time. I seem to remember it was an old Ford, but that was before my interest had been kindled. Coco the Clown brought it over from America and, although there's no documentary evidence, they are pretty certain it belonged to the Keystone Cops. Coco the Clown then sold it to Pierre Picton, who had *Chitty Chitty Bang Bang*. When he retired, I think in the nineties, he then sold it on. The car is still working after 100 years and still entertaining kids when it comes out.

'We took it to Kop Hill and had the ejector seat working and had some actors, including Haurel and Lardy [Laurel and Hardy lookalikes]. The seat jammed up about four feet above the windscreen and the guy sitting on it lost his sense of humour. It wouldn't come down. The crowd was roaring but he genuinely lost his rag. We couldn't get the thing down. Pierre Picton was a great character as well.'

Pierre Picton was a clown who appeared on

BELOW **Pierre Picton demonstrating the pneumatically operated rising driver's seat on his 1924 Model T Ford 'Clown Car'.**
(Ten Tenths)

children's television in the 1960s and '70s and who died in 2016. In his obituary in *The Guardian* newspaper, his nephew David Renton wrote:

He had a favourite prop, a black Ford Model T. Pierre would try to open one door but the opposite door would open instead. He would try again and the right doors would open this time but fall to the ground. Miming, between each setback, incredulity, defeat and renewed hope, Pierre would attempt to drive the car from its back seat. The car would start, before spilling him to the floor.

The car is now part of the Ten Tenths collection, owned by musician and car collector Nick Mason, as Mike Hallowes of Ten Tenths explains. 'We knew of the Clown Car for some time as it had been on the books of Ten Tenths as being available for film and TV work,' he says.

'Latterly Pierre Picton's wife urged Pierre to sell the car as she was worried about him hurting himself in his senior years carrying out the act. He had previously broken his leg with the car by running himself over when it was in self-drive mode! Consequently, Pierre got in touch with us to see if we might buy the car. As Nick remembered seeing the car as a child at Bertram Mills Circus, the idea of adding it to the collection appealed to him. I was sent down to Stratford on Avon, where Pierre lived, to view the car. Not only did I view it but Pierre gave me a private performance of his act with it in the local car park, luckily without further injury to himself! Needless to say, Nick bought it.'

According to Mike, this unique Model T features the following special effects: doors fall off; driver's seat shoots into the air on a pneumatic ram; squirts out water; rear of car tips over, ejecting passengers; various exploding devices using 12-bore blanks to be used during door fall offs, etc.; exploding pigeons on front where headlamps would be shoot 20ft in to the air; various noises (football rattle to sound like engine problem and siren); one front wing opens and shuts like an alligator; the car can start apparently remotely by placement of various switches around the vehicle; ability to start and stop on its own via timer switches; tape player and loudspeaker.

BELOW Pierre Picton with his 1924 Model T Ford Taxi, or 'Clown Car'. *(Ten Tenths)*

Speedsters

By 1913 an extensive aftermarket had developed, providing a wide range of custom accessories, many designed to give the Model T a more sporty appearance. Speedster conversions provided an alternative to the more expensive Mercer Raceabout and Stutz Bearcat options available at the time.

The Speedster often featured a lowered chassis and an extended (or sometimes shortened) wheelbase, together with a 'hotted-up' engine kit consisting of an overhead valve conversion, balanced crankshaft and side- or up-draft carburettors. The body featured a monocle windscreen, and lightweight wire wheels replaced the standard heavy wooden ones.

'By the 1920s there were lots of, by their standards, old Model Ts worth very little around,' explains Chris Barker. 'People stripped off the bodies, lowered them and fitted a Speedster body, which you could buy. The cheapest way to go Model T driving these days is to get yourself a chassis, put a seat and a fuel tank on it and drive it.'

Hot rods

During the 1950s, long after the last Model T Ford had rolled off the production line in 1927, the vehicle acquired a new lease of life in the form of the 'hot rod'.

The person credited with building the first 'T-bucket' hot rod was Norm Grabowski, an American hot rod builder and actor, who used heavily modified parts from both a 1922 Model T touring car and a Model A pickup truck in his creation, along with a Cadillac V8 engine. Grabowski used 6in (15cm) spacers at the rear of the car to give it a highly raked appearance. It became known as the 'Kookie Kar' and featured in the television programme, *77 Sunset Strip*.

'Some people don't like hot rods but the Model T has been used as the basis for them since the teens,' says Neil Tuckett. 'As soon as the Model A engine came out, they stuck one of those in, then when the V8 came out in the early thirties, it wasn't long before they were putting that in a T chassis, but soon after that they went to a Model A chassis because that was stronger.'

ABOVE Advertisement for Model T Speedster body by the Motor Truck Body Company, 1916. *(Alamy)*

BELOW 1923 Model T Ford Street Custom Hot Rod. *(Getty Images)*

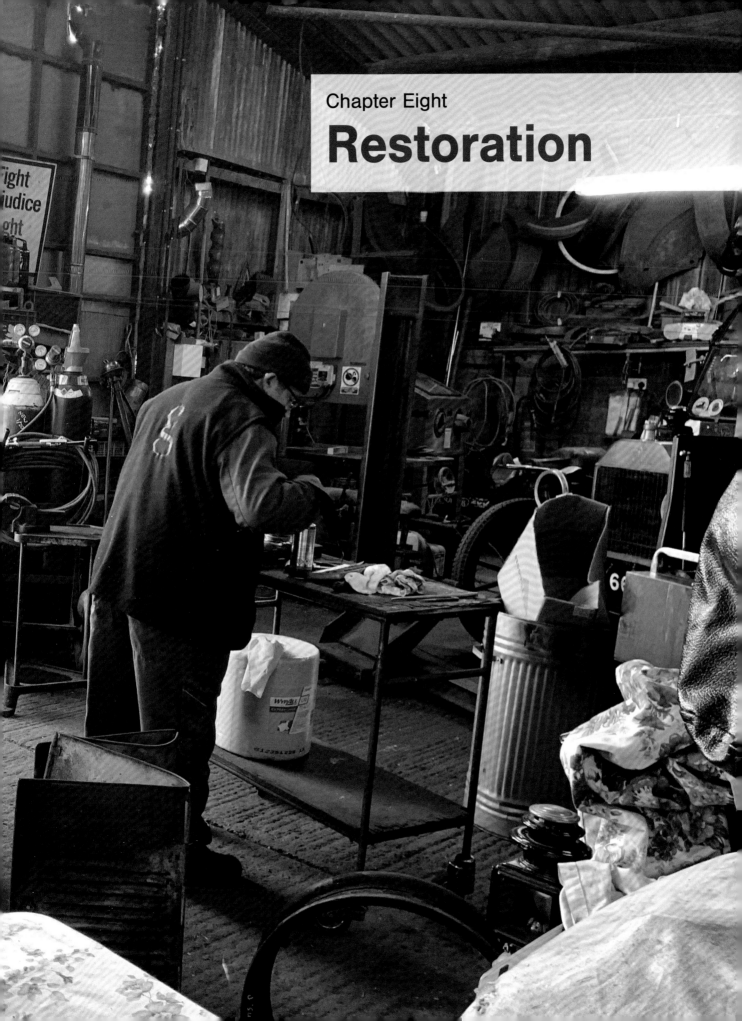

Tuckett Brothers

Tuckett Brothers is one of the UK's leading restorers of Model T Fords, having been in the business for over 30 years, supplying complete cars, parts and literature, and repairing and assisting with anything Model T-related from their workshops in Buckinghamshire.

Owner Neil Tuckett imports a container of spare parts from the USA roughly every six weeks, many of which will eventually be rebuilt into Model T Fords. 'All of those will become a car again,' he says, gesturing towards a pile of chassis frames. 'Because if you've got a chassis you've got a genuine part, and other genuine parts are readily available, as you can see by the amount of axles, engines and that sort of thing. After that, the rest of it is available new.

'When I set up on my own in 1984, in agricultural engineering, one of the first jobs I was asked to do was grind some valves on a Model T Ford. So, I'd always had the interest and always did a little bit of work with them, but the key point was around 1989–91 – we were doing a lot more, because there was no work on the farms. By that time I'd collected a lot of spares and people would ring up – with many old car groups, you can't get many spares unless you swap them. With the Model T, that wasn't an issue. It was a case of finding

PREVIOUS SPREAD, BELOW AND RIGHT

Tuckett Brothers' workshop is an Aladdin's cave of everything Model T, with a number of cars being worked on at any one time. *(Author)*

them and there was so much of it, we were happy to sell.

'I bought a spare engine for myself and a few years later bought another. And two became four and four became ten. I think the biggest heap of stuff I bought in America was 40 tonnes, which was in one scrapyard. I went over to Minneapolis and brought it back.

'A couple of years ago a chap rang me up from North Dakota, he heard that I bought Model T engines, and was I interested? "They're just blocks with a few crankshafts, no other bits with them, no heads but you've got to buy them all." I said, "That's fine." We sat and negotiated and, to cut a long story short, he said he wanted a bit more than scrap value. We agreed a price of $25 a block. I asked how many he had and he repeated, "You've got to buy them all." It turned out he had 820 blocks – 14 tonnes. I told him, "I sell about three a year and that includes Europe, because they don't wear out. I have no idea what I can do with 800 blocks," and the worst thing was, the best stuff had been picked, I assume it's somewhere in America still. So that gives an idea of the quantities of spare parts we're still dealing with.

'They've lasted because of the sheer number that they built, the quality of them and the fact that America never really scrapped anything. Until recent years, when they've been going through with mobile crushers, the outback, as it were, of America was so big no one bothered. They were put in woods or in the fields and sheds and left, and that's where they stayed. They're still coming out of sheds now, three or four generations down. There are still big piles. That has gone in the UK now, though. I'd suggest there aren't many big piles we don't know about over here now. The guys who collected in the fifties have gone and the next generation have either continued with them or sold them, so English stuff is reasonably scarce.

'We're unusual,' he continues. 'I would describe ourselves as a working museum, and if we've got a chassis we can be very green and we can build that car back up from genuine parts and new wear parts. That ranges from, literally, just a chassis with a few heavy iron parts, to an original car that wants stripping and restoring, so you've got the whole range. It is quite common to build Speedsters today, a Speedster being a rolling chassis with two seats. That was done in the '20s, '30s, '40s, nothing new, and kits were available in America.

RIGHT AND OPPOSITE PAGE
Neil Tuckett describes his business as being like 'a working museum'. *(Author)*

Bodies are still built in America and 80% of a Model T is available new today.

'And that's increased,' he adds, 'because when I started in the '70s and '80s, you couldn't even get head gaskets. Now, there's probably 20 companies in America that are living off the back of the Model T and Model A. That's all they do and there's catalogue after catalogue.

'In the UK, there's only a few of us. The Model T Register is obviously very active and there's myself and a couple of other, smaller dealers who just do Model Ts. It's a niche market. You do not want ten people over here doing it. We're working on probably 1,000 customers in the UK, then you've got a few in Europe as well. There's probably no more Model Ts in Europe than there are in the UK. I guess there's 600 English-built vehicles and probably 3,000 in the UK in total. In America, there's at least 100,000 left.'

When he acquires a Model T, Neil always tries to ascertain its history, if at all possible. 'I bought a Model T pickup in a sale in Reading,' he says, 'looked up its registration, and it had come from the Orkneys. I rang up a guy I know, four fields away, who has family there and he came over. He rang up his mum, in the Orkneys, said "Mum, Neil's bought a little Model T pickup." "Oh", she says, "that'll be the one that left in 1965, I know that car." Apparently,

she'd worked on the estate where it had come from and remembers it leaving in 1965. It came down to Reading and now I've sold it back to the family and it's going back up to Rousay. That's history, when you can do that.'

Neil is also very particular in matching components of cars back together, when they have been swapped around. 'I was involved in a big sale down in Essex, 500 old vehicles which two brothers, the Sharp brothers, had collected in the '60s,' he explains. 'There were 17 Model Ts in there. I didn't buy anything in the sale but afterwards, over the next 18 months, I actually had 11 of those Model Ts back. The Sharp brothers, who had collected them, one bought and one played. The one who played took all the Model Ts to pieces, then bolted them all together, but completely swapped everything around. So there was a 1913 body on a 1927 chassis. It was a total mess.

'Eleven of them I got back over the years and I used to swap them round and correct them. Two annoy me – one's in Ireland and one's in Hertfordshire. There's two to be done one day. It's not new. With a Model T it's easy to change parts over. There's been many like that.'

You would have thought that, after a hundred years or more, there would come a point where original parts were just too old to use, but Chris Barker disagrees. 'We haven't got there yet,' he says. 'Ford's materials were very good. If you go and buy a mid-twenties Chevrolet, the chances are that the switches have just crumbled, because they were made of Mazak, a zinc alloy. But Ford used very good materials. Everybody's heard of vanadium steel, which he used, though not as much as people think he did, because it's not suitable for all applications, but he did use good materials and he did train up his own metallurgist.'

Tudor Wheels

Tudor Wheels Ltd is a company offering full restoration services for Model T Fords, vintage and veteran cars and wheels. It is based in the New Forest and is run by Richard Skinner.

'The restoration and bespoke builds have become such a big part of the business at the moment I'd say it was 50-50 between that and wheel restoration and refurbishment. I also look after a number of veteran cars for some

BELOW Every part will one day be used in the restoration of another Model T Ford. *(Author)*

customers who attend the annual London to Brighton run.

'At the moment [early 2020] I am working on one of the oldest Model Ts in the country, a very early 1910, which has come over from America, and is having an absolute full restoration. I've also got a 1913, a 1915, a 1916, a 1923, I've just had two 1923s and a 1927 leave. There are always plenty of Ts about at Tudor Wheels!

'Generally, if I've got a really rusty Model T that comes in, something that's been dragged out of a barn in the States, to completely strip it, renovate it right through, I like to have it fully restored for the customer in about five to six months. You can't hang around and have these things drag on over a long period of time. And at the same time, you've got to keep everyone happy that there's progress happening so you've got to be working on a number of cars and of course you're going to have some set-backs in between. However, I like to feel that I go above and beyond for my customers to ensure they are completely happy with the car and the service. I am always happy to provide advice and consultation for my customers whenever they need it, which they seem to really appreciate.

'Speedsters are still very popular because they're cheap, cheerful and heaps of fun! It was the beginnings of the hot rod craze back in the twenties. Just like today, back then youngsters liked to adapt and whizz up their cars. In the scrapyards there were lots of Model Ts and a youngster could go down to a scrapyard and for five bucks pick up a rolling chassis. Usually the body was rotten because they didn't preserve the wood in any way, so they would just scrap the body and convert it into a hot rod. If you think 15 million Model Ts were produced, they were easy and cheap to come by. Interestingly, in 1921 there was one day on the production line of Model Ts where they produced more cars in one day than Ettore Bugatti produced in his entire lifetime.

'So there were huge numbers of Ts and there was a massive industry where manufacturers who were not doing particularly well in America – they could be making sewing machines, bicycles, heating radiators – soon realised that they could change their tooling and make accessories for the Model T Fords. That included companies like Laurels who decided to make Speedster kits. So you went down to your local Laurel shop and you paid them a couple of bucks and you bought a lowering kit. You then went and bought your Model T for a few bucks from a scrapyard, you bolted on this lowering kit and you had this hot rod, cheap little Speedster. So that's where the Speedster came in and after that, in the late '20s, the hot rod was developed when the Ford V8 came out and they started dropping those into the early Model Ts. So Speedsters are good fun and are very popular.'

'I was approached by a couple who are First World War historians, and the lady, Emma, was in the FANY, the First Aid Nursing Yeomanry. She was fascinated by a woman called Mrs Bond who personally purchased a Model T Ford in 1915 to make into an ambulance.

'She had a lovely picture of Mrs Bond with her 1915 Model T Ford and they asked if I would be interested in doing a commission build for them, based on that one photograph. I had a rolling chassis and I managed to scale the ambulance from the photo. Of course, the average height for a man in the First World War, 1914–15, was slightly shorter than now, so I had to measure both Emma and Rob to make sure I could build a car that they could use. After much research I built an absolutely perfect replica of Mrs Bond's ambulance, which they named Agatha and used and campaigned all over the world.

'Agatha then went to the Great Dorset Steam Fair and they were asked to take it back again because they were commemorating the First World War. I then decided, just as a bit of a giggle, to build an American ambulance to go alongside Agatha. A British ambulance, like Agatha, was based on a current commercial vehicle Model T chassis from 1915, whereas the American ambulance was built specifically by Ford.

'In 1916, all of the car manufacturers in America were asked by the US government: "Could you produce x number of ambulances and they have to be started next week and we have to have them within a couple of weeks?" No manufacturer was big enough to do it apart from Ford, so he came up with the concept of getting a rolling chassis, which he knew was good, and then designed a crate to transport them to the quayside, and the inside of the crate was marked out with the design for the ambulance body.

'When they were unpacked from the crate, the crate was taken apart, the panels were cut up and then reassembled to be the ambulance body. Then they had somebody daubing the whole thing with paint, so you had them arriving in a crate and a quarter of a mile down the quay they were driving off as ambulances! Quite remarkable... a flat packed ambulance!

'I decided to recreate part of that story and so for the following year's Great Dorset Steam Fair and for the commemoration of the First World War, I built Bertie. He was a 1917 American ambulance. I went along dressed in authentic First World War American gear, and with Emma and Rob, got into the spirit of times past as we had both ambulances representing the British and the American Model T ambulance world.'

BELOW Richard Skinner, in authentic period dress, poses alongside Agatha the Ambulance (left) and Bertie the Ambulance (right) at the First World War commemorative display at the Great Dorset Steam Fair. *(Richard Skinner collection)*

The T Service

As the name suggests, The T Service, run by Richard Rimmer in Oxfordshire, specialises in the servicing and sales of Model Ts, rather than full restorations.

'The value of Model Ts makes it difficult from a commercial point of view to do a full restoration,' he explains, 'because they'll almost always end up costing more than the car's worth. We have done full restorations, but it's more the mechanical side we tend to do. Anything from rebuilding the front or rear axle, or rebuilding an engine, to just general small repairs. We do some bodywork repairs as well, so if someone comes in and says they want all the bolt-on panels repainting, we do that using a paint shop a few doors down.

'We install upgrades, including Rocky Mountain brakes, distributor conversions and alternators. I have a colleague who refurbishes the trembler coils using high-tech test equipment, including an oscilloscope, as they can dramatically affect the performance of a Model T. We can also provide replacement timers and a range of accessories.

'In the past I'd worked on VW Beetles; that was my classic car introduction, and I ended up working with someone on those for a while. With the Model Ts, I was looking for a new opportunity. I'd been working with another specialist for a while because my own car got shipped over to the UK in one of his containers. I worked there probably about 18 months but had the opportunity to start up on my own. Someone offered me some cars from America and that kicked things off. We had our first container with three cars come over and that prompted me to set up a workshop and we started from there. I enjoy the people and the cars, it's just a nice community to work within and that is what prompted me to do it.

'As you can imagine, it's a pretty small market because there aren't masses of Model Ts in the country. At a guess I'd say somewhere between 1,000 and 2,000 of them, so you're never going to get loads of companies doing this. Starting from scratch was always going to be tricky, but I've gone from having one car in the workshop that I was trying to sell to probably having 15 cars in here now, some of which are for sale, some are customer cars and a couple are mine. We seem to have had a run on sales. I think people have been sitting around [during the COVID-19 crisis] for so long, not sure what to do with their money, they're now not making anything on savings, so suddenly we've had a bit of a rush on selling cars. I think people are just thinking, "Sod it, I'm just going to go out and enjoy myself!"

'I want people to see the car for what it is and I try and get photos on the website so people can get a good impression of what they're like before they come to me. If someone is coming a long distance I don't want them to be disappointed when they get here, so if anything I tend to be a bit pessimistic on the descriptions. I'd rather people were happy when they arrived. I've been on the receiving end so

I know what it's like, your face just drops when you get there.

'Being in the business, you tend to get offers of cars and they build up a bit, so I did have a bit of a cull recently but they're building up again. I've got a replica of an English van that I've just finished building. The body was found at Beamish Museum. They'd taken it off a vehicle there because people didn't like driving it and found it awkward to get in and out of, so they converted their Model T into something else and I bought the body from them and put it on another chassis.

'Everyone's heard of a Model T and a lot of people will have seen old black-and-white films with Laurel and Hardy, so it's a car they can relate to. I hesitate to say it's a bit of an icon, but it is. Everyone's heard the story of it being the first production line car and the car that put the world on wheels, and so on. The other thing is the reason I got into it – they are useful. They're not something that you have to trail everywhere and you can only do a few miles, or you can only go to a Sunday show and that's all it does. You can actually use these pretty much as a daily car if you wanted, and I have got customers that do that. Again, the parts supply and the fact that someone can phone me up and I've got parts sitting on the shelf that I can supply to them within a day or so, is a big factor.'

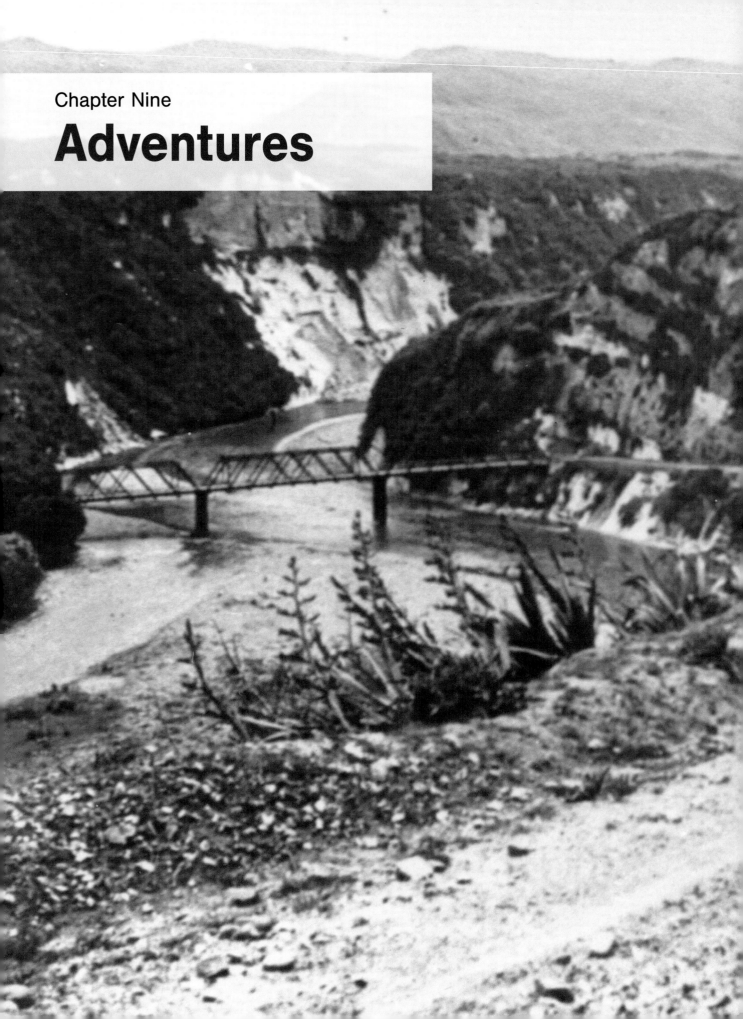

Chapter Nine

Adventures

ABOVE AND
PREVIOUS SPREAD

The challenges of the
rugged New Zealand
North Island terrain
are evident in these
two photographs
taken during the
journey made by
Arthur Chorlton, Harold
Richards and Ernest
Gilling in 1912. *(The
Colonial Motor Company
of New Zealand)*

Across the North Island of New Zealand

The first Model Ts to reach New Zealand arrived in June 1909, and three years later three men set off to attempt to cross the North Island from Wellington to Auckland through a region known as the 'King Country', made up largely of rugged terrain, at a time when there was no known route for much of the journey. They arrived eight-and-a-half days later having covered 500 miles, a journey which was re-enacted 100 years later in 2012 by members of the Model T Ford Club of New Zealand.

The three men were Arthur Chorlton, who came up with the idea; driver Harold Richards; and Ernest Gilling, a press photographer. The Model T Ford was chosen by Chorlton and a car provided by the Colonial Motor Company, which also sponsored the expedition.

The trio set off on Friday, 22 November 1912 from Wellington and reached Taihape at 4.15pm, after covering 142 miles at an average speed of 22mph (35kph). From this point on they were in uncharted territory as far as the motor car was concerned. Two days in they encountered a bridge over a creek that had been washed away but, with help from nearby timber workers, managed to construct a temporary replacement and carried on, reaching Taumarunui that evening.

The following day, the road – such as it was – ran out, with only a grass track to follow alongside the Ongarue River, but later on they discovered that a railway construction team had built a service road and a bridge across the Ongarue valley. Despite heavy rain and a steep climb, the Model T made Matiere by lunchtime. However, soon after leaving Matiere, they became bogged down in the mud and had to call on a farmer and his horses to pull them out. Progress was slow and they only achieved four miles the following day, after which horses again had to be relied upon for assistance from time to time. At the end of the eighth day the trio finally arrived in Hamilton.

The final leg of the trip to Auckland only took half a day, and they arrived at 1.20pm on Saturday, 30 November, eight days and

ABOVE AND LEFT The North Island crossing took the intrepid trio through uncharted territory, involving 'roads' such as those shown in these two photographs that would be challenging even for today's 4x4 vehicles, but the remarkable Model T got the team safely from Wellington to Auckland. *(The Colonial Motor Company of New Zealand)*

13 hours after setting off. The car was then stripped of its equipment and driven back via a more direct route through Taupo, Napier and the Wairarapa in just two-and-a-half days.

John Stokes, author of *Ford in New Zealand – putting the Car before the Horse*, explains: 'The Model T was an important tool for transport development in New Zealand. Unlike Britain, we had comparatively little railway development because of the topography. Roads were also undeveloped, especially in the countryside. The Chorlton trip was inspired by other Ford initiated "adventures" around the world, starting with the Ocean-to-Ocean tour in the US, the trip in Britain to Ben Nevis, and the outback trip in Australia. New Zealand quickly became a main market for Ford: naturally, the US was the biggest market, followed by the production by Ford of Canada, for their domestic consumption and for export to the Commonwealth (except for Britain). Australia was the largest Ford of Canada market, followed by little, wee New Zealand, because the Model T provided so many transport solutions here, which is what the Chorlton trip had set out to promote.'

BELOW Original ascent of Ben Nevis by Henry Alexander in 1911.
(Neil Tuckett collection)

Model T up Ben Nevis

In 1911, Scotland's first Ford distributor, Henry Alexander, decided as a publicity stunt to drive a Model T Ford to the summit of Ben Nevis, at 4,406ft (1,343m), the highest mountain in the British Isles. He tasked his son, Henry Junior with the role of driver and, together with his father and brothers, a week was spent surveying the mountain to select the best route to tackle the ascent. They decided against the standard route used by walkers, from Achintee Farm to Glen Nevis, and instead chose a more gradual ascent from the north side, albeit over bogs.

These proved difficult, but not impossible, to negotiate and the route also took Alexander across a stream and a mountain burn before joining a rocky track, barely wide enough for the car and with a sheer drop on one side. At some corners it had to be bodily lifted around the bend with the assistance of spectators. Snow proved an obstacle near the summit but eventually the observatory at the peak of the mountain was reached on 13 May. The car was left at the summit, with the American and Scottish flags flying over it, while Alexander and his helpers returned to Fort William to join the travelling press.

The following day they ascended, either on foot or horse, and the car, which had been standing at the top of the mountain overnight, was started up without any problems. Alexander began the treacherous descent, albeit with a rope attached to the rear axle to stop the car from running away. The descent took a further two days.

The event attracted great attention from the press; the Glasgow *Evening Citizen* reporting:

Of course, the construction of the car suits the rough work of this kind. There is ample clearance, but stability is assured by a close-set body on a good wheel track. Also, the entire car is wonderfully light for its power, and at last, but not least, the axles have transverse springs, so that they may rock freely, allowing one wheel to rise several feet without any risk of capsize.

ABOVE Henry
Alexander (seated in
car) surrounded by his
team at the summit
of Ben Nevis.
(Neil Tuckett collection)

LEFT Henry
Alexander descending
Ben Nevis in 1911.
(Neil Tuckett collection)

Those who saw the fearful strains to which the chassis was subjected must admit that only material of very extraordinary character could possibly be used in Ford construction. Mr Henry Ford, of whose genius the Ford car is an expression, has made a study of the application of vanadium steel to light car construction, and, it is hardly necessary to add, with great success.

On 12 May 1961, a rally was held by members of the Model T Register to mark the 50th anniversary of the event. It ran from Perth to Fort William and was attended by Henry

RIGHT The Model T
was dismantled to
allow it to be carried
to the top of the
mountain.
(Neil Tuckett collection)

Alexander, a 1910 Model T Tourer being converted into an exact replica of the car in which he had made the ascent.

For the centenary, it had been hoped to recreate the original ascent by driving up the mountain again, but narrowing of the paths, along with the creation of steps, meant that this would be virtually impossible. Instead, an ingenious idea was proposed to build an exact replica of the 1911 car, which could be dismantled and carried to the summit. On 16 May 2011, the team set off and, over the next two days, the car was driven as far as possible through rivers and across bogs up the mountain.

Unfortunately, it had been raining continuously from the moment the party arrived, raising the water table and making the crossings treacherous. Just 500ft short of the halfway point, it was deemed too dangerous to carry on and the car was driven back down to Fort William.

On 18 May the second stage of the ascent commenced. A second car, specially prepared by Neil Tuckett for rapid assembly, was carefully transported by hand by a group of 77 helpers, through freezing conditions. When the summit was eventually reached, it took just 16 minutes to reassemble the car. Later that week it was

moved to the West Highland Museum and subsequently to the Nevis Centre.

Seven years later, on 18 May 2018, a full-size bronze sculpture of the original car, cast at Powderhall Bronze foundry in Edinburgh, was unveiled in the centre of Fort William by Henry Alexander's grandson, Mike Munro.

ABOVE AND BELOW

Despite the appalling conditions, the car was reassembled at the summit of Ben Nevis.

(Neil Tuckett collection)

Appendix

Ford Model T Specifications

(Figures obtained from 'The Essential Buyer's Guide – Ford Model T', by Chris Barker and Neil Tuckett, and 'The Ford in Britain File', by Eric Dymock.)

Car	
Length	12ft (3.66m) (typical Touring Car)
Width:	66in (1.6 8m)
Track:	56in (1.42m)
Wheelbase:	100in (2.54m)
Axle Ratio:	3.64:1
Max Speed:	42mph (68kph)
Weight:	1600lb (725kg) (typical Touring Car)
Engine:	Four cylinders, in-line; L-head side valve; gear-driven camshaft; non-adjustable tappets; detachable cast-iron cylinder head and block; Holley or Kingston updraught single-jet carburettor; low-tension flywheel magneto; low-tension distributor; separate trembler coil for each cylinder; splash lubrication; gravity fuel feed; three-bearing crankshaft
Bore:	3.75in (95mm)
Stroke:	4.0in (102mm)
Capacity:	177-cu in (2,896cc)
Max power:	20bhp @ 1,600rpm
Max torque:	85lb ft @ 1,100rpm
Fuel capacity:	10US gal, 8.3Imp gal, 38 litres (typical Touring Car)
Oil capacity:	1US gal, 0.83Imp gal, 3.8 litres
Transmission:	Rear-wheel drive; epicyclic two-speed and reverse gearbox
Gear ratios	
Low:	2.75:1
High:	1:1
Reverse:	4:1
Chassis:	Straight steel channel-section
Suspension:	Transverse leaf springs front and rear with radius rods
Body:	Various styles, two or four-seats
Equipment:	1909–1915 - no electrical system; 1915–1919 – 8-volt headlamps and horn from flywheel magneto; 1919–1927 – dynamo and battery for 6-volt starting and lighting.
Production:	15,007,003 in USA and Canada; worldwide approx. 16,500,000.
Ton Truck (as above except)	
Length:	16ft (4.9m) (depending on body)
Width:	68in (1.73m) (depending on body)
Track:	56in (1.42m)
Wheelbase:	124in (3.15m)
Axle ratio:	5.17:1 or 7.25:1
Max Speed:	33mph or 24mph (53kph or 39kph)
Weight:	2,200lb (998kg) (depending on body)

Model T specification for 1910

(as given in account of Ocean-to-Ocean Race by one of the crew of car No. 1)

Motor – Four-cylinder, four-cycle, vertical, 20hp, 3¾in bore, 4in stroke. Cylinders cast in one block with water jackets and upper half of crankcase integral, water-jacketed cylinder head detachable, fine-grain iron castings.

Valves – Extra large, all on left side and offset

Shafts – Crank and cam non-welded, drop-forged, heat-treated Ford vanadium steel, bearing surfaces ground, cams integral and ground.

Crankcase – Upper half integral with cylinder casting. Lower half pressed steel and extended to form lower housing for magneto and transmission.

Cooling – Thermosyphon and fan.

Ignition – Ford magneto generator, low tension, direct connected to engine drive.

Carburettor – New design, float feed, automatic with dash adjustment.

Transmission – New design Ford spur planetary, bathed in oil, all gears from heat-treated vanadium steel, silent and easy in action.

Lubrication – Combination splash and gravity system – simple and sure. Insures against insufficient or excessive lubrication.

Clutch – Multiple steel discs, operating in oil.

Control – All speeds forward and reverse by foot pedals. Spark and throttle under steering wheel.

Final Drive – By cardon shaft with single universal joint to bevel gears in live rear axle. Ford three-point system (patented in all countries) with all moving parts enclosed in dust proof casing, running in oil.

Front axle – One piece drop forging in I-beam section, specially treated vanadium steel.

Steering – By Ford reduction gear system, irreversible.

Brakes – Two sets: (a) Service band brake on transmission controlled by pedal; (b) Internal expanding brakes in rear hub drums controlled by hand.

Wheels – Artillery wood type. Hubs extra long.

Tyres – Pneumatic; rear 30in x 3½in, front 30in x 3in.

Number of passengers – Normal load touring car, five adults.

Springs – Front and rear, semi-elliptic.

Fenders – Enclosed full length of car.

Wheelbase – 100in. Tread 56in; 60in for Southern roads where ordered.

Gasoline capacity – 10US gallons. Cylindrical gasoline tank mounted directly on frame.

Weight – Touring Car, 12,200 lbs.

Price – Prices will include top, windshield, speedometer, gas lamps, generator, three oil lamps and horn on touring car at $950.00, Tourabout at $950.00 and Roadster at $900.00. For oil lamps and horn only, deduct $75.00. The Coupé at $1,050.00, Landaulet at $1,100.00 and Town Car at $1,200.00, includes three oil lamps and horn.

Index

Index

Also published by Porter Press International

Ultimate Series
John Fitzpatrick Group C Porsches – The Definitive History
Works 956 Porsches – The Definitive History
McLaren F1 GTR – The Definitive History
Ferrari 250 GTO – The Definitive History

Great Cars Series
No. 1 – Jaguar Lightweight E-type – The autobiography of 4 WPD
No. 2 – Porsche 917 – The autobiography of 917-023
No. 3 – Jaguar D-type – The autobiography of XKD 504
No. 4 – Ferrari 250 GT SWB – The autobiography of 2119 GT
No. 5 – Maserati 250F – The autobiography of 2528
No. 6 – ERA – The autobiography of R4D
No. 7 – Ferrari 250 GTO – The autobiography of 4153 GT
No. 8 – Jaguar Lightweight E-type – The autobiography of 49 FXN
No. 9 – Jaguar C-type – The autobiography of XKC 051
No. 10 – Lotus 18 – The autobiography of Stirling Moss's '912'
No. 11 – Ford GT40 – The autobiography of 1075
No. 12 – Alfa Romeo Monza – The autobiography of the celebrated 2211130
No. 13 – Bugatti Type 50 – The autobiography of Bugatti's first Le Mans car
No 14 – Shelby Cobra Daytona Coupe – The autobiography of CSX2300

Exceptional Cars Series
No. 1 – Iso Bizzarrini – The remarkable history of A3/C 0222
No. 2 – Jaguar XK120 – The remarkable history of JWK 651
No. 3 – Ford GT40 MkII – The remarkable history of 1016
No. 4 – The First Three Shelby Cobras
No. 5 – Aston Martin Ulster – The remarkable history of CMC 614
No. 6 – Maserati 4CLT – The remarkable history of chassis no. 1600
No. 7 – Ferrari 250 LM – The remarkable history of 6313
No. 8 – Ferrari 250 GT SWB – The remarkable history of 2689
No. 9 – Ferrari 857S – The remarkable history of 0578M
No. 10 – Alfa Romeo T33/TT/3 – The remarkable history of 115.72.002

Porter Profiles
No. 1 – Austin Healey – The story of DD 300
No. 2 – Jaguar D-type – The story of XKD 526
No. 3 – Jaguar XK 120 – The story of 660725

Coachbuilt Cars
No. 1 – Jaguar XK120 Supersonic by Ghia

Bespoke books
The Le Mans Model Collection 1949-2009 (three-book set)
Derek Bell – All my Porsche races
DB4 G.T. Continuation – History in the making
One Formula, 50 years of car design – Gordon Murray
The Self Preservation Society – 50 Years of The Italian Job
ROFGO Collection
JUE 477 – The Remarkable History & Restoration of the World's First Production Land-Rover
ROFGO Collection
The Light Car Company Rocket
SuperFinds
Ferrari 250 GTE
The Michael Turner Collection

Scrapbooks
Stirling Moss Scrapbook 1929-1954
Stirling Moss Scrapbook 1955
Stirling Moss Scrapbook 1956-1960
Stirling Moss Scrapbook 1961
Graham Hill Scrapbook 1929-1966
Murray Walker Scrapbook
Martin Brundle Scrapbook
Barry Cryer Comedy Scrapbook
Mini Scrapbook
JCB Scrapbook

The Jaguar Portfolio
Ultimate E-type – The Competition Cars
Jaguar E-type – The Definitive History (2nd edition)
Original Jaguar XK (3rd edition)
Jaguar Design – A Story of Style
E-type Jaguar DIY Restoration & Maintenance
Jaguar XK DIY Restoration & Maintenance
Saving Jaguar
All-American Heroes and Jaguar's Racing E-types

Deluxe leather-bound, signed, limited editions with slipcases are available for many titles. Books available from retailers or signed copies (of most titles) direct from the publishers.

To order, simply phone +44 (0)1584 781588, visit the website or email sales@porterpress.co.uk

Keep up-to-date with news about current books and new releases at **www.porterpress.co.uk**